THE SPANISH CIVIL WAR

Studies in European History

Series Editors: John Breuilly
Julian Jackson
Peter Wilson

Jeremy Black	*A Military Revolution? Military Change and European Society, 1550-1800*
T.C.W. Blanning	*The French Revolution: Class War or Culture Clash?* (2nd edn)
John Breuilly	*The Formation of the First German Nation-State, 1800-1871*
Peter Burke	*The Renaissance* (2nd edn)
Michael L. Dockrill and Michael F. Hopkins	*The Cold War 1945-1991* (2nd edn)
William Doyle	*The Ancien Régime* (2nd edn)
William Doyle	*Jansenism*
Andy Durgan	*The Spanish Civil War*
Geoffrey Ellis	*The Napoleonic Empire* (2nd edn)
Donald A. Filtzer	*The Krushchev Era*
Mary Fulbrook	*Interpretations of the Two Germanies, 1945–1990* (2nd edn)
Graeme Gill	*Stalinism* (2nd edn)
Hugh Gough	*The Terror in the French Revolution*
John Henry	*The Scientific Revolution and the Origins of Modern Science* (3rd edn)
Stefan-Ludwig Hoffmann	*Civil Society, 1750–1914*
Henry Kamen	*Golden Age Spain* (2nd edn)
Richard Mackenney	*The City-State, 1500-1700*
Andrew Porter	*European Imperialism, 1860-1914*
Roy Porter	*The Enlightenment* (2nd edn)
Roger Price	*The Revolutions of 1848*
James Retallack	*Germany in the Age of Kaiser Wilhelm II*
Geoffrey Scarre and John Callan	*Witchcraft and Magic in 16th- and 17th- Century Europe* (2nd edn)
R.W. Scribner and C. Scott Dixon	*The German Reformation* (2nd edn)
Robert Service	*The Russian Revolution, 1900-1927* (3rd edn)
Jeremy Smith	*The Fall of Soviet Communism, 1985–1991*
David Stevenson	*The Outbreak of the First World War*
Peter H. Wilson	*The Holy Roman Empire, 1495-1806*
Oliver Zimmer	*Nationalism in Europe, 1890–1940*

Studies in European History
Series Standing Order ISBN 0–333–79365–X
(outside North America only)

You can receive future titles in this series as they are published by placing a standing order. Please contact your bookseller or, in case of difficulty, write to us at the address below with your name and address, the title of the series and the ISBN quoted above.
Customer Services Department, Macmillan Distribution Ltd
Houndmills, Basingstoke, Hampshire RG21 6XS, England

The Spanish Civil War

Andy Durgan

palgrave
macmillan

© Andy Durgan 2007

All rights reserved. No reproduction, copy or transmission of
this publication may be made without written permission.

No paragraph of this publication may be reproduced, copied or
transmitted save with written permission or in accordance with
the provisions of the Copyright, Designs and Patents Act 1988,
or under the terms of any licence permitting limited copying
issued by the Copyright Licensing Agency,
90 Tottenham Court Road, London W1T 4LP.

Any person who does any unauthorized act in relation to this
publication may be liable to criminal prosecution and civil
claims for damages.

The author has asserted his right to be identified as the author
of this work in accordance with the Copyright, Designs and
Patents Act 1988.

First published 2007 by
PALGRAVE MACMILLAN
Houndmills, Basingstoke, Hampshire RG21 6XS and
175 Fifth Avenue, New York, N.Y. 10010
Companies and representatives throughout the world

PALGRAVE MACMILLAN is the global academic imprint of the
Palgrave Macmillan division of St. Martin's Press, LLC and of Palgrave
Macmillan Ltd. Macmillan® is a registered trademark in the United
States, United Kingdom and other countries. Palgrave is a registered
trademark in the European Union and other countries.

ISBN-13: 978-1-4039-9516-2
ISBN 10: 1-4039-9516-8

This book is printed on paper suitable for recycling and made from fully
managed and sustained forest sources. Logging, pulping and manufacturing
processes are expected to conform to the environmental regulations of the
country of origin.

A catalogue record for this book is available from the
British Library.

A catalog record for this book is available from the Library of Congress.

Library of Congress Catalog Card Number: 2007021660

10   9   8   7   6   5   4   3   2
16   15   14   13   12   11   10   09   08

Printed in China

For Isa

Contents

Contents

List of Abbreviations

AMA	*Agrupación de Mujeres Antifascistas* (Communist-led women's organisation)
BOC	*Bloque Obrero y Campesino* (Workers' and Peasants' Bloc)
CEDA	*Confederación Española de Derechas Autónomas* (Catholic conservative party)
CNT	*Confederación Nacional de Trabajo* (anarcho-syndicalist trade union federation)
CTV	*Corpo di Truppe Volontarie* (Italian expeditionary force)
ERC	*Esquerra Republicana de Catalunya* (Catalan left-wing republican party)
FAI	*Federación Anarquista Ibérica* (Federation of radical anarchist groups)
FET	*Falange Española Tradicionalista de las JONS* (Unified fascist party)
FJS	*Federación de Juventudes Socialistas* (Socialist youth)
FNTT	*Federación Nacional de Trabajadores de la Tierra* (Socialist Land Workers' Federation)
JSU	*Juventudes Socialistas Unificadas* (Unified Communist–Socialist youth organisation)
JAP	*Juventud de Acción Popular* (CEDA youth)
NIC	Non-Intervention Committee
NKVD	*Narodnyi Komissariat Vnutrennich Del* (Soviet secret service)
PCE	*Partido Comunista de España* (Spanish Communist Party)
PNV	*Partido Nacionalista Vasco* (Basque Nationalist Party)
POUM	*Partido Obrero de Unificación Marxista* (Dissident communist party)
PSOE	*Partido Socialista Obrero Español* (Spanish Socialist Party)

List of Abbreviations

PSUC	*Partit Socialista Unificat de Catalunya* (Catalan Communist Party)
ROWAK	*Rohstoffe und Warren Enkaufgesellschaft* (German state import company)
SF	*Sección Femenina* (Falange women's organisation)
SIM	*Servicio de Inteligencia Militar* (Republican secret police)
TUC	Trades Union Congress
UGT	*Unión General de Trabajadores* (Socialist trade union federation)

Editors' Preface

The Studies in European History series offers a guide to developments in a field of history that has become increasingly specialised with the sheer volume of new research and literature now produced. Each book has three main objectives. The primary purpose is to offer an informed assessment of opinion on a key episode or theme in European history. Second, each title presents a distinct interpretation and conclusions from someone who is closely involved with current debates in the field. Third, it provides students and teachers with a succinct introduction to the topic, with the essential information necessary to understand it and the literature being discussed. Equipped with an annotated bibliography and other aids to study, each book provides an ideal starting point to explore important events and processes that have shaped Europe's history to the present day.

Books in the series introduce students to historical approaches which in some cases are very new and which, in the normal course of things, would take many years to filter down to textbooks. By presenting history's cutting edge, we hope that the series will demonstrate some of the excitement that historians, like scientists, feel as they work on the frontiers of their subject. The series also has an important contribution to make in publicising what historians are doing, and making it accessible to students and scholars in this and related disciplines.

JOHN BREUILLY
JULIAN JACKSON
PETER H. WILSON

Chronology

1923–30	Primo de Rivera military dictatorship
1931	
11–14 April	Fall of the monarchy and declaration of the Second Republic
11 May	Burning of religious buildings in Madrid and other cities
28 June	Elections: victory of the Republican–Socialist coalition. Manuel Azaña becomes Prime Minister.
9 December	New constitution approved.
1932	
19–21 January	Anarchist uprising in Baix Llobregat
10 August	Attempted military coup
9 September	Agrarian Reform and Catalan Autonomy Statute approved.
1933	
11 January	Casas Viejas: 21 peasants shot dead by police during anarchist uprising.
30 January	Hitler becomes Chancellor of Germany.
23 April	Partial municipal elections: Centre-Right victory
19 November	Elections: Centre-Right victory. Radical Party government established under Alejandro Lerroux. The *Bienio Negro* (Two Black Years) begins.
9 December	Anarchist uprising: Catalonia and Aragon

1934

12 February	Dolfuss represses Austrian Socialist uprising.
28 March	Workers' Alliance formed in Asturias.
1 June	Catalan Cultivation Contracts Law vetoed by Constitutional Tribunal.
5 June	Farm workers strike in south.
3 October	CEDA enter the government.
4 October	Revolutionary General Strike
4–17 October	Asturian Commune

1935

3 May	Gil Robles becomes minister of war.
October	Mass meetings in support of Azaña
October–December	Corruption scandals undermine Radical Party.

1936

16 February	Elections: Popular Front victory
March	Land occupations begin in south.
14 March	Falange illegalised.
April–July	Fusion of Communist and Socialist Youth (JSU).
8 May	Azaña elected President.
June–July	Strike wave in Madrid and elsewhere
12 July	Assassination of Calvo Sotelo

CIVIL WAR

17–18 July	Military rebellion begins in Spanish North Africa.
19–20 July	Rebels defeated in Barcelona and Madrid.
23 July	Military Defence Junta formed.
25–27 July	Hitler and Mussolini decide to aid rebels.
14 August	Rebels take Badajoz.
4 September	Largo Caballero becomes prime minster of Popular Front government.
9 September	First meeting of the Non-Intervention Committee
15–18 September	Stalin decides to send military aid to the Republic; the Comintern decides to organise the International Brigades.
24 September	CNT and POUM join Generalitat.

28 September	Franco relieves Toledo.
30 September	Plá y Daniel, Bishop of Salamanca, issues pastoral letter supporting the Nationalist 'crusade'.
October	First International Brigade volunteers arrive. Popular Army formed to replace militia.
1 October	Franco becomes head of the Nationalist army and government. Basque Autonomy granted by the Republican government.
25 October	Republican gold reserve shipped to the USSR.
4 November	CNT enters government.
6 November	Republican government moves to Valencia.
7 November	Battle for Madrid begins.
16 November	Hitler sends Condor Legion.
18 November	Germany and Italy recognise Franco.
19 November	Durruti killed in Madrid.
20 November	José Antonio Primo de Rivera executed.
6 December	Mussolini decides to send CTV expeditionary force.

1937

6–28 February	Battle of Jarama
7 February	Fall of Malaga
8–18 March	Battle of Guadalajara
30 March	Rebel offensive in north
19 April	Forced unification of rightist parties
19 April–31 May	NIC naval patrols.
26 April	Guernica destroyed by German and Italian planes.
3–8 May	Street fighting in Barcelona
17 May	Juan Negrín becomes Prime minister.
3 June	Death of Mola in air crash
16 June	POUM made illegal.
19 June	Bilbao falls.
21–22 June	Andreu Nin murdered.
22 June	Special espionage tribunals created in the Republican zone.
1 July	Collective Letter from Spanish Bishops endorses Franco.

6–26 July	Battle of Brunete
6 August	SIM created.
7 August	Private religious ceremonies permitted again in Republican zone.
10 August	Anarchist-dominated Council of Aragon suppressed.
24 August	Republican offensive in Aragon. Battle of Belchite.
26 August	Santander falls.
28 August	Vatican recognises Nationalist government.
10 September	Nyon Conference
21 October	Fall of Asturias
29 October	Republican government moves to Barcelona.
14 December	Republican forces begin Teruel offensive.

1938

30 January	Franco names his first Cabinet.
22 February	Franco re-takes Teruel.
6 March	*Fuero de los Españoles* promulgated by Nationalist government.
10 March	Nationalists launch offensive in Aragon.
16–18 March	Massive bombing raids on Barcelona
17 March–13 June	French border re-opened.
5 April	Prieto dismissed from Republican government.
15 April	Franco's forces reach the Mediterranean, cutting the Republic in two.
16 April	Anglo-Italian agreement
1 May	Negrín's 13-point programme of war aims
24 May	Vatican establishes full diplomatic relations with Franco.
25 July	Republican army launches offensive across the Ebro.
18 August	Franco rejects all peace initiatives.
29 September	Munich Conference.
4 October	International Brigades withdrawn from the front.
16 November	Battle of the Ebro ends.
23 December	Nationalist offensive in Catalonia begins.

1939

26 January	Barcelona falls.
1 February	Republican Parliament meets for the last time on Spanish soil.
9 February	Franco issues retrospective Law of Political Responsibilities making Republican political activity illegal.
10 February	Catalonia falls. Thousands flee over French border.
27 February	Britain and France recognise Franco.
5 March	Casado coup in Madrid
24 March	Franco refuses to negotiate peace with Casado.
27–28 March	Madrid occupied.
1 April	Franco announces war is over.

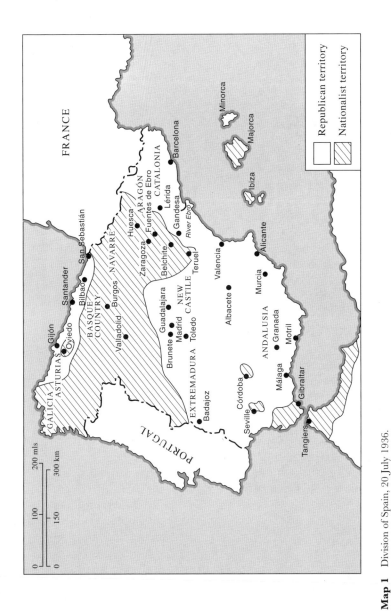

Map 1 Division of Spain, 20 July 1936.
Adapted from G. Esenwein and A. Shubert, *Spain at War: The Spanish Civil War in Context, 1931–1939* (London: Longman, 1995).

xvii

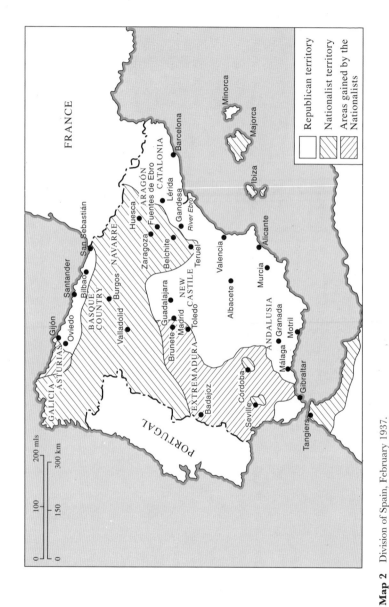

Map 2 Division of Spain, February 1937.

Adapted from G. Esenwein and A. Shubert, *Spain at War: The Spanish Civil War in Context, 1931–1939* (London: Longman, 1995).

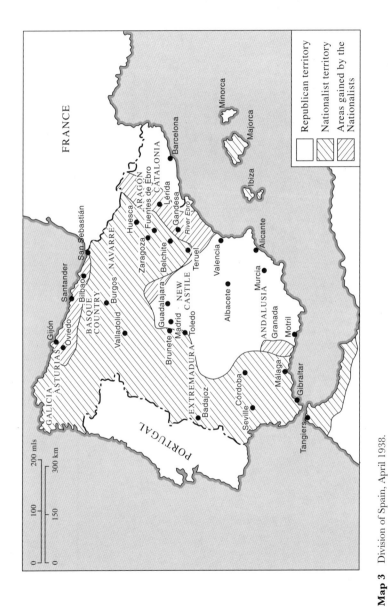

Map 3 Division of Spain, April 1938.

Adapted from G. Esenwein and A. Shubert, *Spain at War: The Spanish Civil War in Context, 1931–1939* (London: Longman, 1995).

xix

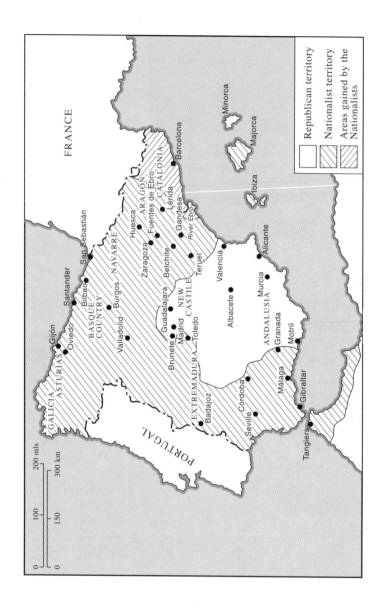

Map 4 Division of Spain, March 1939.

Adapted from G. Esenwein and A. Shubert, *Spain at War: The Spanish Civil War in Context, 1931–1939* (London: Longman, 1995).

Introduction

The Spanish Civil War was one of the pivotal events of the twentieth century. For many it was the prelude to the Second World War, for others the 'last great cause' where the prevailing ideologies of the time entered into battle. For many Spanish people, a time of tremendous hope, even the dawning of a new just world, descended into a nightmare of suffering and death. General Francisco Franco's regime would out-live the defeat of his fascist and Nazi benefactors to become Western Europe's longest surviving dictatorship (1939–75). His very survival was one of the main reasons why controversy and interest provoked by the Civil War has generated such a massive historical literature. This continues to be the case, with a wide range of specialised monographs, as well as updated introductory and longer histories, being published in recent years [54, 58, 63, 71, 74, 75, 77].

This current text, as part of the Studies in European History series, aims to combine a brief outline of the course of the Civil War with a critical introduction to both developments in research and the principal debates posed in recent studies. The balance and range of scholarship referred to aims to cover as many different aspects as possible. To help the reader follow the questions that emerge, this includes mainly publications in English of the last decade or so. A few older studies are referred to where relevant. The inclusion of a limited selection of texts in Spanish tries both to fill the gaps where there is nothing yet published in English and to be representative of current work by scholars in Spain and elsewhere.

The historiography of the Civil War has reflected developments in Spain over the past seventy years, as well as changing trends in historical research at a more general level [53, 55, 60, 61, 63]. Not surprisingly, given the profound socio-political polarisation which led to and was generated by the conflict, the first histories and memoirs of the war were partisan in outlook. Among the defeated in exile, the settling of accounts between the different estranged factions worked against the emergence of a coherent Republican version of the war. In Spain itself, the victors' view of the war became the justificatory ideological cornerstone of the new regime. History was written by state functionaries and its relation to fact was very tenuous indeed [53, 196]. In the 1960s, foreign historians, particularly English speakers, began to challenge the distortions of regime propaganda. These histories were intellectually rigorous and written from a broadly pro-Republican standpoint [56, 58, 77, 140].

The appearance of these highly credible versions of the war's history, combined with limited liberalisation due to Spain's economic expansion, led the regime to modify its view of recent history [53, 73, 196]. While not abandoning a militant and simplistic anti-Communist viewpoint, a more nuanced historiography now presented the conflict as a mutually destructive 'war of brothers', a moment of 'collective insanity'. This view of a shared guilt for the horrors of the Civil War subsequently underpinned the transition to democracy in the late 1970s. The leaders of Spain's democratic opposition were convinced that it was expedient for the sake of stability and peace to draw a veil over the recent past [53, 73]. This was the so-called *pacto de olvido* (pact of forgetting) or *silencio* (silence); a *de facto* agreement under which past crimes and past divisions would be overcome and forgotten.

This 'pact' did not, however, mean that historical research somehow ceased. With the advent of democracy and academic freedom, there was an outpouring of empirical research by, often young, Spanish historians. The following years saw a diversification away from the grand narratives of the mainly foreign hispanicists into more specialised monographs. However, political and institutional histories still predominated, although the emergence of both local and oral history marked an important methodological step forward. The weakness of this new historiography was a tendency to adopt a non-interpretive approach with an emphasis on ever vaster accumulations of data – a reaction, in part, to the previous official control of access to the 'truth' [60]. Foreign historians also took advantage of the new openings for research. While political and diplomatic histories were the most common areas worked on, some scholars, once more principally English speakers, began to venture more into social history [12, 28, 29, 40, 43, 168].

Introduction

During the past decade, work on the Civil War and its origins has diversified further and new methodological approaches have gradually won ground. In particular, the cultural history of the conflict has attracted more attention. Thus questions such as gender, everyday life, community and identity have begun to be studied in more depth, leading to a more multi-layered view of the war [14, 20, 24, 60, 162, 169, 182, 183, 199]. Within this context, 'history from below', whereby working-class life is studied in its spatial and cultural dimensions rather than just through its organisations, has begun to make headway. Parallel to these new directions in Civil War historiography important research in more traditional areas has appeared. This is especially the case in relation to the international dimensions of the Civil War with the opening up of the Soviet Union archives [89, 102, 114, 118, 120] and the return of the debate about the internal politics of the Republican zone, in particular a critique of the supposedly Cold War-inspired parameters of some earlier histories [61, 71, 153].

Memory and commemoration, as elsewhere, have also become a central part of this more diversified understanding of the period [53, 73, 160, 195]. The fact that there was no 'defascistisation', as in post-war Italy or Germany, meant that in Spain, rather like in Eastern Europe, there was a 'suspension of memory' [60]. With the consolidation of democracy and the passing of time, fear began to be overcome. Private memories now could move into the public domain more easily. Also a new generation was not afraid to pose the questions its parents had been afraid to ask. The effective end of the 'pact of silence' in the late 1990s has led to a belated and limited recognition of the victims of the dictatorship. Historians and institutions have taken numerous initiatives to encourage the recuperation of both collective and individual historical memory. The locating and excavation of mass graves containing the remains of victims of right-wing terror are essential aspects of this process [195]. Conservative opinion has greeted this new-found interest in the Civil War by encouraging a wave of so-called 'revisionist' histories that blame the Left for the war, so reclaiming the heritage of the pre-democratic Right [33, 67, 68].

Historiographical diversification has provided a far more nuanced view of the war and its causes, so much so that it is possible to speak of there having been 'a series of Spanish wars' [71] or a 'war of cultures' [63]. This is clearly an advance on the bi-polar view of the 'two Spains', often presented in earlier histories, whereby a 'liberal, progressive and secular' Spain was locked in mortal combat with a 'traditional, conservative and Catholic' Spain. Recent historiography has begun to speak of there being 'three Spains'; the third being that which sided with neither contender and attempted to steer a centre course [38, 76]. But it can be argued that the 'third Spain' was not the centre, whose influence was fairly inconsequential, but a 'revolutionary Spain'. Unlike the centre, which vacillated between conservatism and reformism, the revolutionary movement posed a radical, if diffuse, alternative to both. As Enrique Moradiellos points out, three political models emerged in post-First World War Europe: democratic reformist, reactionary authoritarian and revolutionary collectivist [68]. All three were present in Spain – which in itself challenges any idea of Spanish exceptionalism. Awareness of the existence of these 'three Spains' helps understand the political and military dynamics of the Civil War.

Behind these contrasting ideological models were conflicting class interests. Recent historiography, however, stresses that gender, national identity and, especially, religion cut across class in 1930s Spain. Without wanting to minimise the complexities involved, it is worth making a few brief observations that help contextualise the role of class in the origins and course of the Civil War. For instance, while women had a subordinate role to men across the social spectrum, inter-class resistance to gender-based discrimination was uncommon [152, 162, 191]. National identities appeared to supersede class at a political level as both sides in the Civil War tried to legitimise themselves as the true defenders of a progressive or reactionary model of the 'Spanish nation' [24, 69]. But neither Spanish nationalism nor minority nationalisms had much support among the traditional base of the labour movement. In Catalonia the nationalist movement was divided on a left–right basis, which paralleled class divisions over social reform. In contrast, in the Basque Country there was a cross-class nationalist movement [13, 44, 170]. Religious faith was the main sphere where class difference was apparently not so central, given that the Catholic peasantry in general backed the Right and the military uprising. None the less, the Church's role as guarantor of the existing social structure and the rights of property placed it firmly as an institution on the side of the rich and powerful [7, 29, 174].

4

In the years leading up to the Civil War, defence of class interests determined the oligarchy's opposition to even the most minimal reform that might have impinged on its privileges and power. Likewise, important sectors of organised workers sought to redress generations of social injustice by proposing the overthrow of capitalism altogether, especially once the obstacles to reform became evident. The inability of the political centre, or even the left-wing liberal parties, to impose gradual and limited reform was principally due to their lack of social, economic and political leverage. In contrast, the oligarchy – backed by the ideological clout of the Church – had behind it the economic power of the great landowners and industrialists and an important section of the officer corps. Opposed to this, not so much in the institutions of the new democracy but in the streets, in the factories and on the land, was the great mass of workers and peasants. It was these masses, and not the liberal Republican parties, that provided the backbone of opposition to the military uprising. The lack of an effective liberal democratic alternative shows how the eventual crushing of the revolution of 1936 was central to the Republic's defeat. Finally, the new regime established after 1939 was aimed at perpetuating and guaranteeing the maintenance of the socio-economic status quo. The consolidation of the most extreme forms of capitalist exploitation was the context within which all fundamental civil and political rights were denied to the Spanish people for nearly forty years.

This current study of the Civil War attempts to provide an introduction to both events and pertinent scholarship by taking a basically chronological and thematic approach, thus integrating different historiographical perspectives within the narrative. It also draws attention to certain neglected and marginalised aspects. Most studies of the Civil War, apart from general histories, tend to focus on its origins, military history, the international context and developments in the two opposing zones. This study is also divided between these principal, though not mutually exclusive, thematic areas.

While there is general consensus among historians about the long-term structural origins of the war, historical discussion has centred on whether the war could have been avoided and who, if anyone, was responsible. The specific agendas of parties and their leaders have long conditioned general theses about the origins of the war, and are only now giving way to a more multi-faceted view.

In relation to the military history of the war, the main arguments continue to be over strategy and tactics. New research has clarified the logistical nature of foreign intervention, the arms trade and lessons, if any, learnt by other armies and states. All historians agree on the importance of foreign intervention: the debate is over its genesis, motivations and quantity, and the degree of its centrality to the development and outcome of the conflict. As regards the Republican zone, the polemic over the relation between the revolution and the war is still at the heart of much historical writing. The question remains whether there really was any political and military alternative open to the Republican side other than the Popular Front strategy, and to what extent loyalist policies were conditioned by the Soviet Union. Likewise, it is also pertinent to ask why the revolutionary Left was incapable of consolidating its influence. There has been less work on the Nationalist zone, in part because of the lack of reliable archive material, but also because historians have centred their attention on events in the opposing zone and the international dimension. This weakness in Civil War historiography is now being corrected and questions such as the anatomy of the regime, the degree of responsibility held by the Church, and whether Franco's emerging regime was fascist, can now be better answered.

Without precluding further work in various fields, this book attempts to deal with some of these questions and to draw, where appropriate, some conclusions.

1 Towards War

The Challenge of Modernisation

The task confronting the liberal reformers who found themselves suddenly in power in Spain in the spring of 1931 could not have been more daunting. Their professed aim was to drag their country into the twentieth century by modernising both its economic and its social infrastructures. Their inability to achieve this aim, and the corresponding 'failure' of Spain's first democracy, the Second Republic (1931–6), has often been presented as having led directly to the Civil War. However, it is important to stress that the long-term structural problems were so profound that any programme of parliamentary reform alone was faced with immense obstacles.

The apparent backwardness of early twentieth-century Spain led some to conclude, particularly inside the powerful socialist movement, that Spain had not completed its 'bourgeois revolution' [8, 23, 55, 75]. By this they meant that the basis for capitalist development had not been put in place: the emergence of a strong industrial bourgeoisie, the ending of feudal relations in the countryside, the definitive separating of Church and state and the establishment of a liberal parliamentary democracy with its corresponding political and civil rights. The industrial bourgeoisie was indeed weak compared with its British or French counterparts. Its power was very localised: centred on steel, shipbuilding and mining in northern Spain, or the textile industry of Catalonia. Its very weakness had made the Spanish bourgeoisie particularly insecure and deeply conservative in political matters – in which it was more interested than in economic questions. Labour protest was usually met with extreme intransigence by the employers. But the failure to eliminate the threat represented by the workers' movement or to overcome their economic problems led most industrialists to welcome

General Miguel Primo de Rivera's military dictatorship (1923–30) [4].

During the 1920s, however, Spain modernised more than is often assumed. Nowadays, most historians agree that Spain had indeed become a capitalist country, although with a series of grave structural problems, at least by the turn of the century if not before [10, 23, 48, 71]. Spain did not experience a classic bourgeois revolution in which the structures of the *ancien régime* were shattered. By the end of the nineteenth century the legal basis of capitalism had been established, but without there having been a corresponding political revolution. The country's economic expansion, partly as a result of the boom enjoyed by Spanish industry during the First World War, had led to a rapid increase in its urban population. By 1930, those engaged in agriculture had dropped to under half the working population and an expanded industrial working class would prove particularly susceptible to calls to mobilise for both improvements in living standards and social justice. Other signs of progress were the steady decrease in the death rate and the fact that literacy rose during the 1920s to levels similar to those of France and Italy [45].

Nevertheless, Spain's economy remained relatively backward compared with most of its neighbours, a result not just of the dominance of agriculture but of the very nature of the agrarian system [30, 42, 48]. Forms of land ownership and technological backwardness were both impediments to economic progress. The situation was particularly problematic in southern Spain in the areas of the great landed estates, the *latifundia*, where 2 million landless day labourers, *braceros*, worked on average only half the year and lived in direst poverty. Attempts to modernise agriculture and alleviate rural misery would be at the centre of the clash between Left and Right during the years leading up to the war. It was no coincidence that after 1939 a central plank of the new regime was the maintenance of the pre-Republican rural property structure. Spain's Civil War could therefore be defined as an 'agrarian war', fought and won for the *latifundistas* [37].

The Church, despite the forced sale of its lands in the nineteenth century (disentailment) [8, 48], still retained enormous power. According to the Population Census, there were 113,290 members of the clergy in a population of 23 million by 1931 [45]. The Church's economic power was matched by its ideological influence, in particular through its control over education. The fact that the Church was widely identified with the defence of wealth and privilege was the principal cause of widespread anti-clericalism. Alienation from the Church was particularly strong among the urban working class and the southern rural masses [29]. Violent attacks on Church property had become part of social revolt well before the coming of the Republic and the passing of legislation aimed at curbing clerical power [34].

Along with the landowners and the Church, the other main component of Spain's ruling oligarchy was the army. The failure of the Spanish bourgeoisie to establish strong institutions meant the army had a disproportionate influence and during the early nineteenth century had become the arbitrator of the country's political life, intervening frequently to change governments. Apart from the latent threat of military intervention, there was also an urgent need for structural reform. A top-heavy command structure and promotion not based on merit were, in addition to any technological weaknesses, the main targets of reformers. Compared with other countries, the middle classes were hostile to the army and tended to buy themselves out of military service. This had led to a lack of reserve officers and a correspondingly large and permanent officer corps whose social isolation was compounded by a lack of general education. Promotion from the ranks to the officer class was an important path of social mobility. Thus an officer corps closely linked with conservative sectors was likely to oppose any attempt at social or political reform.

In the nineteenth century, liberal administrations, with the active backing of the army, had sought to build a centralised state, but Spain's historical, geographical and socio-economic fragmentation had proved a serious obstacle to their intentions. Regional identity was particularly strong in the economically advanced and linguistically distinct Basque Country and Catalonia [13, 21, 44]. By the late nineteenth century there was an increasing concern in some intellectual circles about the need to forge a strong Spanish national identity. The emergence of a national media and education system was paralleled by the growth of a modern liberal Spanish nationalism [24, 69].

The long-term structural problems facing any would-be reformers were compounded by two serious difficulties: economic crisis and acute political divisions. Although Spain was not as affected as some countries by the slump of the late 1920s, an over-dependence on exports meant the contraction of the market led to an increase in the number of unemployed and pressure on the already miserable living conditions of the rural poor [30, 37, 42, 48]. The acute political divisions that plagued the new democracy which emerged in 1931 were a clear reflection of the long-term polarisation and fragmentation of Spanish society.

The subsequent undermining of democracy can only be understood therefore within the context of this inter-related and complex set of variables that characterised Spanish society in the first decades of the twentieth century.

The Limits of Reform

A generation of liberal Republicans thus set out to tackle these deeply rooted structural challenges: agrarian and military reform, clerical power, and demands for regional autonomy. While it has been claimed that the Republicans' reform programme was too ambitious, too cautious or even sectarian in its aims, the social and economic weight of their opponents would prove decisive. The reformers were to be confronted by the entrenched interests of an extremely conservative oligarchy and the fears of a mass of Catholic peasantry that the existence of both the Church and private property were under threat.

The inability of the Primo de Rivera regime to improve Spain's economic situation was the principal reason why sections of the political elite not only abandoned the dictator but even turned towards republicanism. Likewise, the effective neutrality of the army in relation to both the dictatorship and, in particular, the King, Alfonso XIII, also opened the doors to the Republic [4]. The new democracy that now emerged was the culminating point of a 'process of civil awakening and modernisation' that had constantly been eroding the foundations of autocratic politics since, at least, the First World War [3]. The two pivotal components of the growing reform movement were the middle classes and organised labour. Working-class mobilisation during 1930, often overlooked by historians, undermined the ineffective military government that had replaced Primo in January 1930 [16]. The political expression of the reform movement was the Republican–Socialist pact. The

Republican parties won much of their support from urban professionals and intellectuals. They were divided between progressive reformers on the left and the more moderate factions, in particular the Radicals, on the centre-right. The Radical Party, led by the *enfant terrible* of early twentieth-century Barcelona street politics, Alejandro Lerroux, now cultivated a politically ambiguous image that allowed it to attract support from both the middle classes and recent converts to republicanism from the oligarchy [4]. The Spanish Socialist Party (PSOE) and its union, the UGT, had maintained its organisational infrastructure as a result of having collaborated in the dictatorship's system of labour relations. Although retaining a verbal commitment to revolutionary change, in practice the PSOE was wedded to social democratic gradualism. Most importantly, it saw collaboration with the Republicans as opening the way to the long-overdue bourgeois revolution in Spain which in turn would establish the prerequisites for the gradual introduction of socialism.

Ruling-class ineptitude and growing popular mobilisation provided the opportunity for the Left to impose a Republican administration in the wake of its victory in the municipal elections of 12 April 1931. The declaration of the Second Republic on 14 April was met with massive celebrations and great hopes of social and political change among the urban working and middle classes. Awareness of these expectations and the failure, in large part, to meet them, is important if the subsequent problems and eventual débâcle of the Republic is to be understood.

The new Republican administration's first task was to organise elections to establish a Constituent *Cortes* (parliament), which in turn would elaborate a constitution. The elections of June 1931 confirmed the ascendancy of the Republican–Socialist coalition. The Right, having not recovered from the débâcle of the dictatorship, was reduced to a small minority inside the Cortes; but it would soon become clear that the Left's parliamentary majority alone was not sufficient to carry through its ambitious programme of reform. The coalition was undermined first by the Radicals, who promptly revealed themselves as more interested in becoming the reference point for conservative opinion than for social and political change. By December 1931 they had broken with the Republican–Socialist coalition, hence making the left Republican parties dependent on the Socialists. The debate over the new constitution clearly revealed the problems the government would face. The clauses referring to the separation of Church and state faced sustained opposition both from the rightist minority and from the President of the Republic, the moderate Catholic Nieto Alcalá Zamora. However, the new constitution was unacceptable to Spanish conservatives, not so much because it was anti-clerical but because it was liberal and democratic [36].

Not all reform failed. A massive school-building programme was undertaken during the Republic, and basic literacy improved significantly, particularly in rural areas [11, 24]. The promotion of popular culture, education and progressive social legislation meant the situation of women in Spain also began to change. Despite the reluctance of the Republicans to grant female suffrage because of fears that women would vote for the Right, the new democracy provided women with political and social rights for the first time, thus ending, formally at least, their status as second-class citizens [152]. The slow but steady inclusion of women in the urban labour market in both industry and services had already begun to lay the material basis for undermining this traditional role, although in rural areas these changes were less marked [6, 41]. Conservatives opposed most attempts to provide popular and secular education, seeing it as a waste of money and fearing that such cultural programmes could only lead to a break-down in the natural order of things. The Right and the Church organised their own array of cultural organisations, especially to inculcate youth in a traditionally conservative view of the world. Right-wing and Catholic interests tried to counter even the limited changes in women's status by stressing, wherever possible, their mission in life as mothers and wives [24, 50, 199].

The most sustained and damaging opposition the Republican government was faced with was over its agrarian and religious reform. The Left was determined to extenuate the distress of the southern masses by providing both minimal labour rights and the redistribution of land. In the countryside itself, the disastrous olive harvest of the winter of 1930–1 made conditions even worse for the landed poor and exacerbated class hatred. Poverty was such that two-thirds of the rural workforce would qualify for settlement under the Agrarian Reform provisions. The fears of landowners were soon confirmed when the measures introduced had 'unexpected revolutionary implications' [37]. The *latifundista* system depended on the existence of large numbers of landless labourers on very low wages, thus any increase in wages or protection against dismissal would undermine its whole structure.

From the outset, the Right in the Cortes did everything possible to hold up the Agrarian Reform legislation, repeatedly submitting multiple amendments. Outside parliament there was little machinery to enforce decrees. Related legislation such as the Law of Municipal Boundaries, which prevented the hiring of outside labour, the Eight-Hour Day and the establishment of Labour Arbitration Committees (*Jurados Mixtos*) was also effectively sabotaged by local authorities, working closely with landowners and backed, more often than not, by the paramilitary rural police force, the Civil Guard.

The separation of Church and state, the removal of the clerical control of education and the disbanding of the Jesuits, as well as the introduction of civil marriage and divorce, all provided more ammunition for the Right. Religious reform also meant ecclesiastical wealth became state property and religious orders were prohibited from being involved in business. The withdrawal of crucifixes from schools and the suppression of religious processions, in particular, led to intense resentment. Such measures alienated an important sector of the population from the Republic and led to religious identity becoming a major factor in undermining democratic reform [7, 34, 50, 187]. The Catholic Right mobilised thousands of the faithful by linking the defence of religion to the defence of property. On the left, in contrast, hostility towards the Church as an institution cannot be separated from constant clerical support for the most conservative sectors of Spanish society and its opposition to Republican democracy from the outset [29, 174]. For instance, the nationwide outbreak of church burning in May 1931 was provoked by a monarchist meeting in Madrid rather than any specific action by the ecclesiastical authorities, thus illustrating the close connection in popular consciousness between the extreme Right and the Church.

Military reform was based on a view of what an army should be like in a liberal bourgeois society. The structure of the army was rationalised and all its judicial functions were taken away. In order to reduce the over-manned officer corps, officers were offered retirement on full pay, and promotion on merit was introduced. Sections of the military hierarchy saw such changes as betraying the ideals of the army as the safeguard of traditional values, and most studies suggest it contributed to the army's willingness to rebel. Nevertheless, the problem with the army was not so much resentment caused by military reform as the ideological orientation of many officers, which meant they would prove very susceptible to the same issues that inflamed right-wing opinion in general during the Republic [1].

Given that the defence of national unity was one of the central tenets of Spanish conservative thinking, it was to be expected that the granting of the Catalan Statute of Autonomy in 1932 would upset the military. The Statute conceded some control over domestic affairs and won widespread support in Catalonia itself. Catalan nationalism's roots were similar to those of other modernising nationalist movements that emerged in nineteenth-century Europe. The first Catalan elections, in November 1932, resulted in the left-wing Republican *Esquerra Republicana de Catalunya* (ERC) beating its conservative rivals of the Lliga to take charge of the regional government, the Generalitat. In contrast to its Catalan counterpart, Basque nationalism was backward looking and had race as one of its core values. The Basque Nationalist Party (*Partido Nacionalista Vasco*, PNV) received widespread support from a conservative and devoutly Catholic rural population. Moves towards autonomy in the Basque Country were thereby undermined by the PNV's opposition to Republican reformism and by the Left's rejection of Basque nationalism as reactionary. Although a Statute was finally agreed on, after much acrimonious debate and the withdrawal of Navarre, the election of the Centre-Right government in November 1933 cut the process short [13, 21, 44].

Crisis and Radicalisation

The failure of the reform process led to an underlying crisis that the Republic would never recover from. Conservative historians have attributed this crisis to the Left's actions having alienated small property holders and the Catholic faithful alike. However, the systematic obstruction mounted by a right-wing opposed to all social and liberal reform *per se*, if not the very idea of representative democracy, was decisive. To the government's left, the workers' organisations were increasingly restless about the slow pace of reform.

Towards War

The attempted coup by the head of the Civil Guard, General
José Sanjurjo, in August 1932 was a sign of both the danger posed
by the conspiratorial Right and the continuing ambiguity of
Lerroux, who was accused of being involved in the plot [49]. The
coup's defeat was due to lack of support from the majority of the
Right and a general strike – backed by all the workers' organisations – in the uprising's centre, Seville. Sanjurjo's rebellion had two
effects. First, it encouraged the parliamentary Left to push through
the Agrarian Reform legislation and the Catalan Statute. Secondly
it further radicalised a workers' movement whose increasing disillu-
sion with the Republic would eventually undermine the liberal Left.
The radicalisation of many Socialists and their anarchist rivals is
usually treated as a separate phenomenon but in reality it shared
certain basic premises.

The anarchist movement had emerged in the very distinct socio-
economic contexts of rural Andalusia and industrial Barcelona [20,
143]. Yet in both cases, impoverishment, employer intransigence
and the absence of a political or legal framework for labour relations meant that anarchist methods of direct action and mass
mobilisation appealed to *braceros* and factory workers alike. The
anarcho-syndicalist trade union federation, the *Confederatión Nacional
de Trabajo* (CNT), gave this movement a collective expression, and
the ideologically purer Iberian Anarchist Federation (*Federación
Anarquista Ibérica*, FAI) acted as its vanguard. Recent studies stress
how the anarchist publications and popular cultural associations,
the *Ateneos*, played an important role in working-class education and
leisure [20, 24, 40]. A specifically class-based collective identity
resulted from this cultural context and from the daily experience of
trade union agitation in the workplaces.

Anarchist hostility to the Republic was not immediately palpa-
ble. Not only did the more moderate sections of the CNT leadership welcome the establishment of the new democracy, but,
contrary to what is often assumed, even some of the more radical
anarchists were not initially hostile. The wave of strikes that had
begun by early summer 1931, particularly in Catalonia, had more
to do at this stage with attempts to improve conditions in the workplace and reinstate sacked workers than with any sort of generalised offensive against the Republic. Even the telephone workers'
nationwide strike in 1931 – often presented as a prime example of
anarchist irresponsibility – was for demands that left-wing

15

Republican leaders had also supported prior to the fall of the monarchy. The CNT's subsequent alienation from the Republic was a result of repression directed against the anarchists by the new authorities, employer intransigence, and the privileges afforded by the state to its Socialist rivals. As a result, more militant elements, often from the FAI, won the leadership of the CNT's unions in Catalonia and elsewhere [19, 20, 28, 143].

The new CNT leadership adopted the strategy of 'revolutionary gymnastics' whereby the masses supposedly would radicalise as a consequence of constant mobilisation. The clearest expression of this strategy was three attempted armed insurrections launched over the next two years under different pretexts, and called by relatively few activists without consulting the membership in any serious way [19, 143]. The result of these abortive uprisings was hundreds of casualties and arrests, the closing down of many union centres, a steep decline in dues-paying members and exacerbation of existing divisions in the workers' movement. During the attempted insurrection of January 1933, 21 peasants were killed by the new Republican paramilitary police force, the Assault Guards, in the Andalusian village of Casas Viejas. The resulting scandal was heavily exploited by the Right to undermine the credibility of the Republican prime minister and principal architect of the reform process, Manuel Azaña [38].

The new-found militancy of important sections of the socialist movement had its roots in both frustration with the blocking of the reform process and changes in the nature of its membership. The clearest example of the latter was the massive growth of the Socialist Land Workers' Federation, the FNTT. The social base of the socialist movement now shifted from being mainly skilled workers, particularly in the north and Madrid, to include a volatile mass of impoverished and newly radicalised southern farm workers. What is striking about the local FNTT is that its militancy was similar to that shown by the CNT in the *latifundia* areas, thus suggesting that objective circumstances and social structure had more to do with labour practices than ideology.

The Socialists, like other working-class organisations, were also radicalised by the rise of fascism in Europe and the sympathy it engendered among the Spanish Right. Particularly alarming for the Socialists was the identification of the largest right-wing party in Spain, the recently formed Spanish Confederation of Autonomous

Rightist Groups (*Confederación Española de Derechas Autónomas*, CEDA), with the European authoritarian Right. The systematic and largely effective obstruction of reform inside and outside of parliament by this party would alter the Socialists' perception of the possibility of change within bourgeois democracy [36]. The CEDA, led by José María Gil Robles, was inspired by the encyclicals of Leo XIII on 'accidentalism', whereby what mattered was not whether the regime was a republic or a monarchy but that Catholic interests were defended. Whether the CEDA was an embryonic Christian democratic party [32, 33] or a proto-authoritarian formation [36] is particularly relevant when considering what factors eventually undermined Spanish democracy.

The accidentalists' apparent acceptance of parliamentary legality distinguished them from the 'conspiratorial' extreme Right, whose main components, the Alfonsine monarchists and the Carlists, openly advocated the overthrowing of the Republic. The Alfonsists were influential in upper-class circles, particularly through the journal *Acción Española*, which provided much of the intellectual basis for the extreme Right's rejection of the Republic and liberalism [22]. Carlism, particularly strong in rural Navarre, had its roots in the violent dynastic struggle of the previous century and advocated absolute monarchy and Catholic fundamentalism [5, 35]. In contrast to the conspiratorial Right, since it had been formed in 1932 the CEDA had converted itself into a mass party. The party leadership was dominated by large landowners and urban professionals but among the Catholic peasantry of central Spain it had won widespread support due both to Republican anti-clericalism and to fears that agrarian reform would benefit the landless at their expense.

By 1933, the moderate reform programme of the left-wing Republicans was all but paralysed and the country appeared to be spiralling towards further instability. Parliamentary obstruction had reached such a height that by mid-1933 the Cortes was often barely quorate, given the pointlessness of most debate. The economic crisis, although less catastrophic than in many other democracies, aggravated the situation further. Between 1930 and 1933 unemployment officially affected 12 per cent of the working population, over half in the countryside. The real figure was probably double that, and the situation was made worse because of the absence of any form of welfare provision. Meanwhile, the number of strikes had reached a new high [45].

Faced with the government's paralysis, on 11 September Alcalá Zamora appointed Lerroux to form a new administration. Lerroux's rejection of PSOE participation in his Cabinet meant, effectively, its expulsion from government. In the absence of a viable parliamentary majority, Alcalá Zamora called elections for 19 November 1933.

The new elections would prove a watershed for the fledgling Republic. The Republic's electoral law heavily favoured coalitions and led to a surprising array of agreements, especially on the right and centre. The Radicals' opportunism meant they stood in some constituencies with the CEDA and in others with the left Republicans [15, 25]. The elections brought home how much the political climate had changed in barely two years. The CEDA mounted a massive campaign using the most modern electoral techniques, many directly copied from the Nazis. Its election posters appealed to voters to 'save Spain from Marxists, Freemasons, Separatists and Jews' and its press reminded its readers that Hitler had come to power legally. The Socialist campaign was dominated by its emergent left, in particular the latter's leader Francisco Largo Caballero, the revolutionary tone of whose speeches increased apace with the militant reaction of his audiences. Largo, long-standing leader of the Trade Union Federation (*Unión General de Trabejadores*, UGT), had been minister of labour in the Republican government and was responsible for introducing most of the legislation aimed at improving workers' rights and living standards. The sabotage of his reform was instrumental in pushing him, at least at the level of rhetoric, sharply to the left.

In particular, the 1933 elections exposed the weakness of the left Republican parties as an independent force. Outside Catalonia, the number of left Republican deputies fell from 112 to 14. No left Republican was elected without help from either the Socialists or the Radicals [25]. The defeat of the Left has usually been blamed on the Socialists for having rejected a new electoral alliance with the Republicans [23, 36, 56, 63, 77]. However, a closer look at the elections shows a more nuanced picture. The effects of disunity on the left have been exaggerated. In fact, in over a third of all constituencies joint left-Republican–Socialist lists were presented. On the basis of the actual votes cast for the different lists it is possible to extrapolate that a general coalition would not necessarily have produced a victory of the Left as had been the case in 1931 or would be again in 1936 [15].

The Radicals' behaviour in the elections also guaranteed a rightist victory. Joint centre-right lists led to the election of a quarter of the CEDA's deputies and nearly half of the Radicals' representatives. In 1931, the Radicals had stood as part of the Republican–Socialist coalition and in 1936 their vote collapsed, so the effect of their shift to the right clearly determined the outcome of the elections and the evolution of the Republic over the next two years [15]. Added to this was the vigorous abstention campaign mounted by the anarchists, in contrast with 1931 and 1936. There was a significant decrease in participation in a whole number of constituencies where the anarcho-syndicalists were strong, with the notable exception of Barcelona, and a calculated loss of 500,000 votes for the Left as a result [25, 28]. The fledgling Republic now entered into a period of regression, under the erratic premiership of Lerroux, that would further hasten the country along the road to war.

The Right in Power

The polarisation that characterised Republican politics in 1933 deepened under the Centre–Right government. The Socialists' turn towards extra-parliamentary agitation became even more pronounced and has been blamed for pushing conservative opinion further towards the right. But this avoids placing Socialist radicalism in the context of both massive attacks on the gains made by the labour movement since 1931 and the rise of fascist and authoritarian regimes internationally. This increasing radicalism can be contrasted with the emergence of the Popular Front, which appeared to show mass support for a more moderate Left. Subsequent events would suggest, however, that a more contradictory process was underway.

Lerroux's new government, elected on 'a distinctly conservative agenda' [49], paralysed the reforms of the previous administration. Gil Robles, anxious to avoid new elections, supported the Radicals for the time being. Lerroux may not have been as influenced by the Right as is often claimed [33, 49] but his actions in government failed to convince the Left that this was not the case. From the time of the anarchist uprising in December 1933 through to the crisis of October 1934, there was a near permanent state of emergency. Most strikes were declared illegal and landowners and employers set about reversing any improvements in workers' conditions over the previous two years.

The Socialists rejected the result of the elections, claiming fraud in the south, where the margin of the Right's victory was sufficiently small for this to have led to the Left's defeat. Inside the socialist movement, Largo Caballero's followers had increased their influence, especially inside its youth organisation, the *Federación de Juventudes Socialistas* (FJS), and the UGT. However, this new-found radicalism was not just prevalent among the movement's left; even the PSOE's leading social democrat Indalecio Prieto, despairing that the institutional road was blocked, threatened revolution. This radicalisation was most clearly reflected in the setting up of a joint PSOE–UGT committee to organise an insurrection in the event of any attempt to install an authoritarian regime. The violent crushing of the Austrian socialists in February 1934 by Engelbert Dollfuss, whose reactionary Catholic corporatism resembled Gil Robles's own, provided the Left with a further reason to see the CEDA as the harbingers of fascism.

The threat posed by the authoritarian Right led to the creation of the 'Workers' Alliances against Fascism' involving the Socialists and other workers' organisations. In particular, the small dissident communist Workers' and Peasants' Bloc (*Bloque Obrero y Campesino*, BOC) played a central role in promoting the Alliances [16, 17]. The great weakness of the Alliances was the absence of the CNT, the one exception being in Asturias where the anarcho-syndicalists had always been more favourable to working-class unity [43].

By late September 1934, the CEDA had announced it was no longer prepared to prop up the Radical-led government. Alcalá Zamora named a new government on 4 October, which included three CEDA ministers. The entrance of the CEDA into the Cabinet was a direct challenge to those sectors of the workers' movement, especially the Socialists, which had been promising revolution if the authoritarian Right 'took power'. Gil Robles and the Right knew that this promise was essentially bluff and saw provoking a rebellion as a great opportunity to destroy the workers' movement before it was better prepared [36].

Socialist talk of revolution aimed not only to frighten the Right but also to maintain control over a base whose radicalisation belies the argument that the mass of workers were not interested in revolutionary change [168]. The superficiality of the PSOE and UGT leaders' position had been exposed during the farm labourers' stoppage in June 1934. The Socialist leadership failed to back the FNTT-led strike, arguing that such 'economic strikes' were a waste of workers' energies in detriment to the forthcoming revolution. The systematic ignoring of social laws, the slashing of wages, and Civil Guard brutality meant it was difficult to tell union members in the rural south to be patient. The strike was denounced by the government as 'revolutionary', despite legal procedures having been followed by the union, and the authorities carried out mass arrests, closed premises and replaced Socialist town councils [12, 30]. Without solidarity action from the rest of the socialist movement, the FNTT was easily defeated and would play no part in the forthcoming revolutionary movement.

Faced with the CEDA's entrance into government the PSOE's Revolutionary Committee called an ill-prepared general strike. But the revolutionary rhetoric of the Socialists was not matched by any serious organisational measures. The Revolutionary Committee had drawn up plans for an insurrection but only through Prieto's efforts were some arms smuggled into the country. FJS instructions to form militias had met with little response. Once the strike started, the Committee was promptly arrested, removing even a nominal leadership of the movement. Without the participation of the Socialists' mass rural base in the south, the rebellion was only of any significance in Catalonia, the Basque Country and, above all, Asturias. In Madrid, there was a total lack of co-ordination. The local Workers' Alliance, seen by the Socialist leadership as just a convenient way to control other organisations, did not even meet. Despite sporadic fighting and sniping by the badly equipped and untrained Socialist militia, the would-be insurgents failed to occupy key points in the city. After nearly ten days the movement in the capital collapsed [46].

In Catalonia the movement had a distinct dimension given the conflict between Madrid and the regional government, the Generalitat, over the latter's planned reform of agrarian contract law. Under pressure from the Catalan landowners the law had been declared unconstitutional, leading to threats of separatist rebellion. The Workers' Alliance sided with the Generalitat thus linking the struggle to defend Catalan national rights with the more general labour mobilisation against the Right. Pressurised by the Workers' Alliance in the streets, the Catalan President, Lluis Companys, reluctantly responded to the CEDA's entrance into government by declaring a 'Catalan State within the Spanish Republic'. But given the timid attitude of the Catalan Republicans and the absence of the CNT the movement was soon crushed [16].

The great exception to the movement's débâcle was Asturias, where the miners, along with other workers, held off the attacks of the army for two weeks. The Workers' Alliance took over the region, organising the economy, and its own militia, and imposing revolutionary justice. Adrian Shubert argues convincingly that the crisis in the coal industry was behind the radicalisation of Asturian miners – supporters of the moderate Socialist leader Prieto – rather than any more general commitment to revolution [43]. The specific causes of the miners' militancy thus fed into the more general radicalisation of the workers' movement, regardless of the ideological orientation of its local leadership.

The events of October 1934 would prove decisive in pushing the country towards civil war. For sections of the Left, the bloody repression unleashed on Asturias by the Army of Africa under the command of General Francisco Franco, with hundreds murdered and tortured, was a salutary lesson in what could be expected from the military and the authoritarian Right. The belief that only armed insurrection could avoid counter-revolution became widespread. For the Right, the uprising was a warning of the dangers of revolution and would lead to growing support for conspiratorial factions.

In the aftermath of the October rebellion thousands of suspected participants were imprisoned, workers' centres were closed down and the purge of militants in the workplaces and on the landed estates intensified. For Stanley Payne, compared with repression carried out against the Left by authoritarian regimes elsewhere, what happened in Spain in late 1934 was relatively restrained. The fact that the Left, despite restrictions, continued to organise, also demonstrated the moderation and 'extraordinary tolerance' of the Radical–CEDA government compared with the extremism of their opponents. In fact, more widespread repression could, he claims, have saved the Republic [32, 33]. However, given the persecution of the Left at a local level, the sabotaging of reform, the rise of fascism internationally and the CEDA's sympathy for an authoritarian solution, it was hardly surprising that much of the workers' movement had little faith in a purely institutional defence of democracy.

One of the most important consequences of October was the clamour for unity on the left. For the more moderate elements, the uprising showed the complete folly of pursuing a revolutionary course of action, and strengthened the idea that the only way to avoid the destruction of democracy would be to rebuild the Republican–Socialist alliance. The resulting electoral coalition, soon known as the 'Popular Front', was principally a product of domestic politics [153] despite its obvious similarity to the broad anti-fascist alliances of the same name now advocated by the Communist International (Comintern) in Moscow. For the Communists, the Popular Front represented a radical break with the Comintern's previous ultra-left sectarian line. Behind this radical change of orientation was both a response to the threat posed by the far right to the very existence of the workers' movement and, especially, the need for the USSR to secure an alliance with the Western democracies against Nazi Germany. The defence of democracy, rather than proletarian revolution, would, it was hoped, convince bourgeois governments that a deal could be made with the Soviet Union.

The negotiations to form a left-wing electoral front were initially faced with the left Socialists' opposition to any repeat of the Republican–Socialist alliance. As a condition for accepting a new pact, Largo Caballero demanded the incorporation of the Communist Party. Such a demand can be seen as an attempt to cover up for the fact the left-wing Socialist leaders, despite all their bluster about the need for revolution, had no real alternative to offer to the electoral alliance and therefore needed to give it a radical gloss by including the Communists. The coalition's programme, however, was essentially that of the left Republican parties.

The enforced absence of the workers' organisations from political activity helped the newly united left Republicans gain some credence as the principal public opposition to the rightist government during 1935. This was particularly the case with Azaña, who, along with Prieto, was the most visible advocate of electoral unity on the left. In the autumn of 1935 he addressed several massive rallies the success of which seemed to demonstrate support for a moderate left-wing alternative to the Right [153]. But this assumption overlooks the decidedly radical atmosphere among the crowd at these meetings – the only public forum available at the time [16]. Given subsequent events during the spring of 1936 and at the beginning of the war, it is fairly clear that at least part of the Left's electorate had little sympathy for the liberal agenda offered by Azaña and Prieto.

Meanwhile the Centre-Right government had stumbled from crisis to crisis. The Radicals' attempts to occupy the centre ground of Republican politics had failed abysmally. According to Nigel Townson, this débâcle was due to their collaboration with the anti-Republican Right; their failure to defend the reforms introduced during the previous two years; the personal, if not authoritarian, power of their leader; and their heterogeneous make-up [49]. Radical Party involvement in widespread corruption meant that by December 1935 the government had ceased to function in any real sense, and eventually Alcalá Zamora had no choice but to call new elections for 16 February.

The clash between what seemed to be the 'two Spains' was dramatically acted out in the new elections. The context of the elections was clearly different from 1931. Not only had many leftist voters' hopes of the new Republic been undermined but what was seen as the spectre of fascism appeared to threaten even the minimum gains made by the working class. The Right presented itself in a new and even more strident version of the 'anti-Marxist' pact it had formed in 1933. Now, without the troublesome presence of the Radicals, the authoritarian designs of the CEDA, aligned in a 'National Bloc' with the virulently anti-Republican monarchist parties, were even more explicit. On the Left, in practice, unity was more precarious. The primary objective of every party was to preserve its own identity and, for instance, there was not one joint meeting of the Popular Front [27].

The election result reversed the Left's defeat of 1933. The disintegration of the Radicals and political polarisation meant that most of the centre vote was divided between the Left and Right. The Left also benefited from the absence of any abstention campaign by the anarchists. The Popular Front now faced the task of resuming the reformist project truncated by two years of Centre-Right government.

The Popular Front

The months leading up to the outbreak of war saw both the Right abandon any pretence of respect for democratic legality, and the incapacity of the left Republicans in dealing with either rightist conspiracy or popular demands for radical reform. While civil war was never inevitable, only decisive action against the Left's enemies could have possibly avoided a generalised armed conflict.

The new government was faced with immense difficulties. The problems that had undermined the reformers' modernising programme in 1931 were still in evidence. Apart from the growing extra-parliamentary agitation, the government was weakened by being based on only part of the Popular Front coalition. Inside the PSOE, Largo Caballero's faction blocked any collaboration in government, arguing that the 'bourgeois parties' should carry out 'their' revolution. The Socialists meanwhile would supposedly wait in the wings to install a proletarian government once this stage had been completed. The left Republican parties were further weakened by the fact that their most capable leader, Azaña, replaced Alcalá Zamora as President, thus removing him from direct involvement in government.

Outside parliament, enthused by the electoral triumph, thousands of people stormed the jails and freed political prisoners. In the south, where drought in 1935 had ruined the olive harvest producing acute unemployment and hardship, the FNTT now reasserted its influence. The agricultural workers' federation was not prepared to tolerate any more delays in the process of agrarian reform and began a campaign of land occupations. The conservative offensive of the previous two years was reversed: municipal governments elected in 1931 were re-established and there were attacks on rightist and Church property. The assertiveness and determination of once submissive workers infuriated landowners.

Inside the PSOE, the supporters of Prieto and Largo Caballero effectively functioned as two separate parties. Despite the latter's followers' growing influence over the socialist movement's leadership, among the rank and file the support for one faction or the other was not clear, as the selection of party electoral candidates showed. In prison, after the October events, Largo had supposedly converted to revolutionary Marxism but his motivation, as ever, was to keep control of the rank and file and preserve organisational structures. In fact, most of Largo's supporters wanted to impose a radical programme rather than split the party. The abstract nature of the Left's commitment to revolutionary politics was clearest in relation to the rest of the workers' movement, particularly the CNT. Despite the fact that the anarcho-syndicalists were increasingly open to collaboration with their UGT rivals, proposing in May the formation of a Revolutionary Alliance, Largo did not pursue this offer.

The section of the Left that made most headway in the spring of 1936 was the Spanish Communist Party (PCE). Like many other Communist Parties, the PCE's turn away from the sectarian line of the early 1930s led to its rapid growth. In particular, the Spanish Communists began to influence sections of the left Socialists. The forming of Socialist–Communist liaison committees in many localities and the integration of the Communist trade unions into the UGT facilitated this process. Apart from a number of individual Socialist leaders who would move close to the Communists, this influence was most evident among the leadership of the FJS. During a visit to the USSR in March 1936 it was won over to the idea of forming a united youth organisation with the Communists. The resulting Unified Socialist Youth (*Juventudes Socialistas Unificadas*, JSU) provided the PCE with a mass base, the importance of which would become clear during the war [151].

The appeal of anti-fascism is usually cited as the main reason why the FJS was prepared to unite with the Communists. However, the Comintern's defence of 'one united proletarian party', which coincided with the formal position of the left Socialists, along with the influence of the USSR as the world's only socialist state, were probably more decisive reasons [16]. This is especially relevant when considering the Communists' later influence (see pp. 90–1). The Communists also fused with Socialist groups in Catalonia to form, in July 1936, the Unified Socialist Party (*Partit Socialista Unificat de Catalunya*, PSUC). However, a dissident Communist party, the Workers' Party of Marxist Unification (*Partido Obrero de Unificación Marxista*, POUM), founded in September 1935, was an uncomfortable rival in Catalonia for the PSUC [16, 17, 140, 147].

Upon losing the elections most of the ruling elite abandoned, if they had not already done so, any hope that the Republic could defend their interests, and turned increasingly to the extreme Right [35, 178]. Inside the army, officers who had long opposed the

Republic were now actively plotting its downfall. The Right's electoral failure meant that the military uprising would have quite a broad social base. Direct civilian involvement with the military plot was limited however, the exception being the Alfonsists, who provided crucial finance and liaison for the planned coup.

To justify its stance the Right spread the idea, later consecrated as fact by the post-war regime, that the Left had 'falsified the elections' and the Popular Front government was illegitimate. Claims that the government's Electoral Commission annulled the election of conservative deputies [33] contrast with documentary evidence that indicates that, in fact, it favoured the Right [36]. Backed by its press and the Church, the CEDA now promoted a vision of complete social collapse and chaos. In parliament even Gil Robles's demagogy was eclipsed by that of the Alfonsine leader José Calvo Sotelo, who openly declared himself a fascist and called on the army to 'deal furiously' with the 'enemies of Spain'. Calvo Sotelo's inflammatory speeches were designed, in part, to avoid any reconciliation between more moderate CEDA members and conservative Republicans. In fact, the CEDA would be a major contributor to pushing the country into war. Sympathy for the Nazis had been widespread in its ranks since 1933 [82] and most of its youth organisation, the *Juventud de Acción Popular* (JAP), crossed over *en masse* to the fascist Falange in the spring of 1936. The Falange had been formed in 1933 and had tried to elaborate a specifically Spanish version of fascism containing elements of Catholicism and the concept of 'national syndicalism'. Sustained mainly by the sons of the upper classes, the Falange had had little support until the aftermath of the 1936 elections. Despite this new-found strength, the Falange was still forced to recognise that the only path to power was through the army even though its leader José Antonio Primo de Rivera feared, justifiably as it would turn out, that his party would be subjugated to the military in the event of a successful coup [35, 178, 184, 197].

Increasingly, during the spring of 1936, there were violent clashes on the streets of Madrid and other cities between armed Falange youth and members of the left-wing organisations, creating an atmosphere of pre-civil war. It is misleading, however, to see this violence as a response to 'Republican repression' [33] as this had been one of the Falange's main tactics since its foundation [47]. For the military plotters, the Falange's role was to carry out acts of terrorism and provoke leftist reprisals, and thus justify right-wing propaganda about disorder. Conservative commentators have frequently cited anti-clerical outrages as a justification for the uprising; but recent research demonstrates there were no clergy among the victims of political murder in the months leading up to the war and that the amount of Church property burnt was nowhere near as great as has been claimed [148, 174].

Paramilitary groups, organised by the more radical factions during the preceding years, now became increasingly active. Most were lightly armed and poorly trained and – with the exception of the Carlists and perhaps the Communists – were generally ineffective [2, 47]. These groups' activity made the political situation even more untenable. More significantly, their behaviour reflected what had become a far wider acceptance of a violent solution to the crisis the country faced [68]. It is also worth noting that political parties' youth wings were central to the activities of these paramilitary groups and extra-parliamentary militancy in general. With over 20 per cent of the active population under twenty [42] and only those over twenty-three able to vote, this radicalism was not reflected at an electoral level. Hence evidence that the Popular Front's electoral base tended to favour the more moderate candidates [23] is not necessarily as significant as has been suggested. On the left at least, this divorce between street and institutional politics helps explain the massive impact the 'third', revolutionary, Spain made on events.

In the weeks leading up to the military uprising, in addition to street violence there was a steady increase in strikes, aimed principally at reinstating sacked workers or re-establishing working conditions rescinded by the previous government. According to Stanley Payne, these 'often violent, strikes' were unjustified and aimed 'just to dominate private property' [33]. Other sources show that employers were deliberately intransigent and sought to provoke disputes as part of the general rightist offensive aiming to provide justification for military intervention [23, 27, 36]. The Madrid building workers' strike was indicative of the dilemma facing the Popular Front. Despite appeals from Socialists and Communists to end strikes deemed 'harmful' to the Republic, the capital's 100,000 building workers launched an all-out stoppage in June which, coinciding with a whole number of other disputes, brought the city to a near standstill. Construction had become the biggest industry in the city, in part due to the large number of public works established by the government to palliate the effects of rampant unemployment. The mass of unskilled workers employed in the industry benefited little from the reforms introduced by the first Republican government and were attracted to the CNT as a militant alternative to the more staid trade union practices of the UGT [26, 27, 46]. The CNT's fortunes elsewhere in the months leading up to the war were mixed. The insurrectionary strategy had been highly damaging to its organisation and the CNT's Congress in May, apart from indulging in abstract discussions about future libertarian society, recognised this by calling for working-class unity and emphasising the need to take up more mundane issues [143]. However, while the anarcho-syndicalist unions were gaining new adherents in Madrid and elsewhere, recent studies show that in their Catalan stronghold they faced increasing challenges by rival unions, often led by Marxists, particularly among sections not traditionally seen as militant such as service and white collar workers [16, 17, 19].

Meanwhile, the military plot to overthrow the government continued apace. Not all officers, however, supported the planned coup, which was evidence that at least part of the army had changed during the Republic as a result of reform. The relative ease with which the military rebels plotted is perhaps the most telling testament to the lack of political will of the left Republican leaders, who refused to take preventive action. Despite knowing about the plotters intentions, the Republican government refused to act. In the last analysis, they were shown to be as fearful, if not more so, of the masses as the extreme Right in the army [54, 68]. The killing of Calvo Sotelo on 12 July, itself an act of revenge for the murder of a left-wing captain of the Republican Assault Guards, proved a useful justification for the launching five days later of the military rebellion.

While few historians claim the war was inevitable, there is considerable debate as to how it could have been avoided. It is generally accepted that stronger government action to restore order could have contributed to stabilising the situation. Stanley Payne, in line with current neo-Francoist revisionist histories [67, 68], blames the Left for provoking the war both by its insistence on 'sectarian' reform and by its tolerance of social unrest and even revolutionary violence. Only the moderate liberal centre defended constitutional democracy but the Radicals, the main centre party, were not an attractive alternative because they 'lacked leadership and morality'

[32, 33]. Edward Malefakis, in turn, argues that the possibility of a strong centre emerging was undermined by the left Republican parties' alliance with the Socialists [30, 66]. With an eye on subsequent events in the war, the Republican government has been accused of having carried out the PCE's 'short-term programme' in its aim to repress right-wing opposition and open the way for a Republic of a 'new type' [89, 114]. In this context, the coup was a 'pre-emptive strike' as 'democracy no longer existed'; if it had, Payne argues, there would have been no Civil War. The only real alternatives, he concludes, were a pre-1923 constitutional monarchy or a corporatist CEDA-led dictatorship that would have restored order without going to the extremes that Franco went to [33].

Other historians argue that had Prieto taken over as prime minister a strong reforming government could have been established, which would have both provided hope for the masses and dealt firmly with the military plotters [23, 38, 153]. But the influence of Largo Caballero's faction on the PSOE Executive was an obstacle to any direct participation in a 'petty bourgeois' government. This hypothesis is further undermined by the intransigence of the Republic's enemies. As Paul Preston, one of Prieto's firmest admirers, suggests, a Republican–Socialist coalition under the moderate Socialist leader would have been just as 'intolerable to the rural upper classes', given the Right's 'determination to concede nothing'; Civil War could have been avoided only if the Left had been 'prepared to accept the pre-1931 social structure' [36]. Faced with this alternative, and having learnt from October 1934, the workers' movement and the Left in general opted for resistance. Within a few days, in at least half of Spain, the problems that had confounded Republican reformers would be 'solved' on the streets, on the land and in the factories.

2 The Course of the War

Two Armies

The military history of the war cannot be separated from its political history. Whether Franco, who soon became the rebels' supreme commander, was 'incompetent' or not was secondary to his aim of physically and morally destroying the enemy. On the loyalist, Republican, side the orthodox strategy eventually pursued was determined by the need both to bring under control the revolutionary movement of the early weeks of the war and to convince the foreign powers that the Republic was fighting to defend liberal democracy. Foreign aid, or the lack of it, would be the other decisive factor in determining the war's outcome.

Once the uprising started on 17–18 July, in those major cities where the workers' movement mobilised, the military rebels were generally defeated. The presence of thousands of workers, albeit poorly armed, in the streets, assured in many areas the loyalty of Assault Guards and even the Civil Guard. Where the workers' movement waited for the authorities to take the initiative, the rebels were usually victorious given the Republican parties' reluctance to distribute arms to the civilian population. The immediate territorial division of the country left about 60 per cent of the population and most of the main industrial areas in the hands of the Republic. The rebels controlled some of the more important agricultural areas and had managed to divide the loyalist zone in two, the north being isolated from the centre and east. This geographical division, with exceptions such as Seville and Saragossa, reflected the political division of the 'two Spains': the conservative centre and northwest largely in insurgent hands and the liberal and revolutionary east, south and industrial north controlled by loyalists (see Map 1).

In the peninsula the Spanish army was split more or less evenly

31

between the two sides. What counted, however, was not the quantity of troops but their quality and the material available to them. The Republican government had, in most cases, appointed top commanders it thought reliable, so only four of seventeen serving high-ranking generals backed the rebellion. But most of the officer corps was hostile. Of nearly 9,000 serving officers, just around a quarter remained loyal. Of these, some were Republicans who had been promoted; for others, once they found themselves trapped in the loyalist zone it was pure expediency to obey orders. Many of these officers served the Republic to the end. Others would sabotage the war effort or soon desert to the rebels. The majority of conscripts, who made up the bulk of the army's rank and file, remained loyal if given the opportunity. Despite later right-wing claims that the Republic had more aircraft, this was not the case and few of the pilots available had much flying experience [52, 167]. One exception to the Republic's relative military weakness was that most of the navy remained in its hands thanks to crews swiftly taking over their ships.

As the army did not disintegrate in what became known as the Nationalist zone, existing structures of command and organisation could be used. In August 1936, the rebels had some 160,000 troops at their disposal, including militia, principally organised by the Falange and Carlists. Unlike their Republican counterparts, the rebel militias accepted hierarchical authority without question and thus their integration into the army presented few problems. The Nationalist militia, particularly the largest, the Falange, was mainly used to 'cleanse' the rearguard. Front-line fighting was generally left, especially in the first year of the war, to professional troops such as the Army of Africa and regular Italian forces. Foreign aid was crucial to the rebels' success. Not just the constant supply of arms and material, but also the training and military advice provided by Germany and Italy were both qualitatively and quantitatively superior to anything the Republic received.

Apart from foreign support, the rebel forces had two other main advantages: the quality of their officers, and the Army of Africa. Unlike the Republic, the rebels had an abundance of professional officers to choose from, including those capable of commanding large-scale units. The Army of Africa was so important in the first months of the war that the Nationalists would probably have been defeated without its participation [80]. Commanded by General

Franco, it had some 45,000 men. These included the Foreign Legion and Moroccan units, the only combat-ready troops of the Spanish army, which were used with devastating effect to spearhead the rebels' drive in the south and west of the peninsula.

Nearly 80,000 Moroccan troops fought in the war, playing a central role as the Nationalists' shock troops. Most Moroccan recruits were members of tribes that had traditionally collaborated with the colonial authorities so coercion was limited. The economic rewards, the main motivation for fighting, were quite high in a context where the failed harvest of the previous winter meant that hardship among many peasant families was greater than normal. Ideological pressure was also exerted, both in an appeal to participate in a war of the 'great religions' against the 'atheist' Republic and, even more cynically, through vague promises of autonomy or even independence. Recent research points to other circumstances which encouraged Moroccan participation such as a desire to get revenge for years of humiliation and repression at the hands of the Spanish. The fact that the Republic had done nothing to redress this situation made it easier for the Nationalists to find willing recruits. Evidence of acquiescence with the rebel war effort by Moroccan Nationalists based in the Spanish protectorate challenges the assumption that they were potential allies of the Republic [80, 92, 107]. But the fierce opposition to recruitment in some areas and the 'desperate measures' [107] needed to maintain it suggest that the CNT and POUM's proposal to organise an uprising in Franco's rear was not so unrealistic. This proposal was rejected by the Republican government, however, so as not to upset colonial interests in the region [56, 92].

The military strategy adopted by the Nationalists was essentially conservative. Like their enemies, they were not skilful or experienced enough to draw lessons on the ground or to fight a war of swift movement. In the rebels' favour, the concentration of political and military power helped overcome their initial organisational and strategic weaknesses. Despite this centralised authority, 'considerable latitude' seems to have been given to individual commanders compared with their Republican counterparts, which proved important when the chain of command broke down. This, along with material superiority, often gave the rebels the advantage in spite of frequent resort to the same conservative tactics used by their enemy, of large frontal assaults by waves of infantry [52].

With few exceptions [72], most military historians consider the Nationalist leader General Franco to have been a timid and slow commander, who never carried out a brilliant operation [173]. He was 'a brave and competent colonial officer', largely respected but also feared by his men, of whom he demanded massive sacrifices. The slowness of the war was in fact due to Franco's aim to annihilate the enemy, rather than just his conservatism [185, 186]. This was probably not the case in the early days of the rebellion, when he expected to triumph swiftly, but Franco soon came to the conclusion that a rapid victory would have left intact the basis of future resistance. In this sense, the Nationalists' military strategy cannot be separated from their political programme, at the centre of which was the aim of destroying the Republic's social base, both physically and psychologically. Franco's aim was unconditional surrender, so all attempts to mediate in the conflict would be rejected.

Given that much of the army that remained in the government-controlled zone more or less totally disintegrated, those officers who fought to defend the Republic did so in the hastily organised anti-fascist militias. With around 150,000 troops, the militias were set up principally by the UGT, CNT and other workers' organisations. There were few strictly Republican units, reflecting once more the lower middle classes' relative lack of resolve in combating fascism compared with the proletariat. The militias harnessed the initial enthusiasm of the first days of the anti-fascist struggle. Many were organised on a relatively democratic basis; political discussion was common; 'delegates' or officers were often elected and there were none of the privileges of rank associated with traditional armies. The command of the militia columns was usually in the hands of former leaders of the different pre-war paramilitary formations [2].

Contrary to what many accounts claim, the militia were more likely to be let down by the professional officers supposedly advising them than by any lack of discipline in combat situations [54]. But although the militias stopped the initial advance of the rebel forces, their limitations soon became evident. Apart from the lack of arms, training and experience, the absence of a centralised political and military authority undermined their effectiveness. To remedy this situation, the majority of the Left favoured the establishment of some form of regular army. Even some anarchist military leaders, after experiencing the slaughter of their troops at the hands of a better trained and equipped enemy, soon called for a stricter code of discipline and the establishment of a 'war militia', which would include conscription but remain under the control of the unions. The POUM argued for the creation of a Red Army, based on the experience of the Russian Revolution, which would combine the political and voluntary nature of the militias with a centralised command [140, 147]. However, without a revolutionary political power to back it up, the extreme Left's military proposals came to nothing.

The conversion of the militia into a regular army ('militarisation') was decreed on 30 September 1936. With few exceptions, militarisation was accepted by most militia units [140, 154, 163]. The latter were converted into units of the new Popular Army, usually with the same commanders, now with a formal rank. Conscription was also introduced and a centralised high command established. The new army replaced the egalitarian, democratic and voluntary nature of the militia with more traditional forms of military discipline and hierarchy. It differed from a traditional army in that the political allegiances of the former militia often remained intact inside the new army units. Moreover, the appointment of Political Commissars charged with maintaining the troops' morale, ideological formation and welfare also appeared as a break with military orthodoxy and clearly mirrored the Soviet model.

The Republic also faced great logistical and organisational difficulties. Massive and swift transfers of men to threatened parts of the front were exacerbated by the bad state of roads and railways. Brigades, divisions and corps were set up without the benefit of existing administrative organisation or bases. Units might be formed on paper, often without arms, or officers to command them. In theory, divisions were commanded by senior officers, usually recently promoted from the infantry, while brigades were often headed by former militia officers, and battalions by new men. Unlike the rebel army, there was a real absence of officers with infantry combat experience on the Republican side. Lower-level commanders, often from a non-infantry background, were less aggressive than their Nationalist counterparts and tended to be 'very conventional and unimaginative' [54]. The absence of initiative shown by Republican officers has been attributed to both a lack of training and the conservatism of commanders, who insisted on keeping a tight control over lower ranks [52]. Worse still, while competent officers were sometimes overlooked because of political bias inside the General Staff, others were given commands beyond their capacity. The rapid creation of training schools only partly helped overcome the low quality of Republican officers. It was not until January 1938 that former militia officers were allowed to advance beyond the rank of major, even though some of them were already commanding divisions and army corps.

There was no clear Republican military strategy until mid-1937 [57]; in part because of the lack of any recognised authority that could have carried one out. Republican military theory, like that of the Nationalists, was based on French concepts following the experience of the First World War. So although well supplied with tanks initially, the Popular Army used them in dispersed units to support infantry, in accordance with French teachings, rather than in concentrated attacks. The Republican air force and navy were also handled indecisively.

The capacity and limitations of the new army would soon mark the character and development of the war. Once organised it was shown to be capable of launching effective and, at times, devastating offensives which repeatedly threw back the Nationalists' forces. However, a pattern was soon established whereby the Popular Army was unable to follow up these attacks owing to the lack of reserves and equipment. The overwhelming superiority of the rebel army would then impose itself and the lost ground would be regained, all at a terrible cost for both sides, but with the difference that the Republican army had far greater difficulty in replacing its losses in both men and material. Moreover, while the creation of the Popular Army undoubtedly helped the Republic stem the Nationalist advance in the short term, the elimination of the radical spirit of the militias would remove a powerful motivation for rank-and-file combatants in what would always be a very unequal struggle [56, 62, 140, 163]. An indication of the commitment of the former militia was that its leaders, often commanding through example, were among the most effective officers in the Popular Army.

The Republic's military strategy was subordinated to the government's political orientation. In order to maintain middle-class support at home and win over the democracies abroad, the Popular Army had to be presented as an 'orthodox' army. A restricted use of the navy, to avoid alarming the imperial powers, is one of the clearest examples of the consequences of this orientation [52]. On land, for the Republic to fight a well equipped regular army such as Franco's, it either had to have at its disposal a similar force or use irregular methods of warfare. An alternative strategy would have been to have fought a largely defensive war punctuated by multiple and rapid incursions by both regular troops and guerrilla units into the sparsely defended parts of an extremely long and under-manned front. Such a strategy, Antony Beevor argues, would have given the Republic the possibility of holding out until the European war began, as its declared military aim later became. It would have tied down large numbers of Nationalist forces and avoided the massive destruction of loyalist troops and material, which eventually undermined the Republic's ability to resist. Guerrilla actions, however limited by repression, could have mobilised political sympathy in the enemy rearguard in support of subversion [54].

Other historians dismiss the option of guerrilla warfare, either as unfeasible owing to the massive support for the rebels in the enemy rearguard [66], or as a pointless hypothesis because the Republican government was convinced that it could win an orthodox war and that there was no alternative to a strategy based on the perspective of gaining support from the democracies [153]. Guerrilla warfare was also never developed because after the First World War such methods, even to the anarchists, seemed out-of-date [57]. For others, the fact that guerrilla tactics were hardly used, despite suitable terrain, was due to the political priorities of a Republican government determined to keep tight control over the army and hence avoid the mass radicalism that had characterised the first months of the war. The rejection of large-scale guerrilla warfare was one more example of how the loyalists discarded potentially feasible strategic alternatives in order to convince foreign democracies of the non-revolutionary nature of their struggle [52, 54, 62].

From Coup to Civil War

The first phase of the war lasted from July 1936 through to the spring of 1937. During this time the Nationalists conquered about half the country (see Map 2). What had helped turn 'a coup going wrong into a bloody and prolonged civil war' [185] was Hitler's and Mussolini's decision to send aircraft to help transport the Army of

Africa across the Straits of Gibraltar in the first great military airlift in history. Within a week the rebels were receiving regular supplies of arms and ammunition from the fascist powers. It was not just foreign aid that tipped the scales in the rebels' favour in the south, but also the passivity of the Republican navy, hamstrung not only by fear of German and Italian air power but above all by the Republican government's aim of not upsetting Britain and France. The British authorities' refusal to grant facilities in Gibraltar to the Republican fleet further undermined any attempt to prevent the rebels crossing the Straits. The fleet's eventual transfer to Cantabria was, as Michael Alpert states, 'maybe the major (military) mistake of the war' [51, 52].

A 'colonial style war' was the only experience that Spanish generals had, but in the first weeks this was used to great effect in the south, with the Army of Africa moving in relatively mobile columns as it swept through the south-west of the country securing occupied territory by the widespread and calculated use of terror (see p. 106). Faced with its small but highly trained units, the militias were easily put to flight in open countryside. Frontal assaults by the rebels on enemy positions tended to be avoided, with the exception of the attack on Badajoz. It has been suggested that Franco's decision to turn back to Badajoz was a strategic error because it gave more time to the Republicans to organise their defences elsewhere. But the most likely explanation is that it reflected his caution and he wanted to link the two zones under rebel control [185]. He also now had unrestricted access to Portugal, which, along with the proximity of their North African base, would prove decisive at this stage for the Nationalists' war effort.

The relief of the Alcázar of Toledo, held since the beginning of the war by several hundred Civil Guards and officers, proved very important in boosting Franco's image as providential leader of the Nationalist cause. The reality of the heroic defence of the Alcázar was more squalid. The plight of hundreds of hostages, many chained in the cellars, was never mentioned [100, 196]. If Franco had not diverted his troops and had proceeded straight to Madrid, he probably would have taken the city as its defences were still being organised and outside aid had yet to arrive. In fact, Franco mistakenly believed that Madrid's defences would not be improved.

Madrid had held out in part because the other main Nationalist army, headed by General Emilio Mola, in the north, had been forced to divert troops to San Sebastian and Aragon. Meanwhile, the pace of the advance from the south had slowed down by September because the loyalists were now better organised. Crucial to the Republic's survival, along with the gradual reorganisation of its armed forces, was the decision in mid-September by the Soviet Union to send military aid.

Arming the Popular Army was a central problem for the Republican authorities throughout the war. Despite a steady increase in home-produced material, the Republic remained dependent on foreign arms. The loyalists did possess, however, the fifth largest gold reserve in the world, and the Air and Navy minister Indalecio Prieto mistakenly believed it would provide the possibility of unlimited resistance [95]. Most histories have centred their attention on the sending of this gold to the USSR, thus overlooking that the Republican government had already authorised on 24 July the sending of about a quarter of it to Paris to buy arms. Even though France soon stopped selling war material to the Republic, the gold continued to be sent, to be used to purchase military hardware on the open market, until March 1937.

In September, with Madrid threatened by the rapid advance of the Army of Africa, it was decided to send the remaining gold to the Soviet Union. The Republic sent its gold reserve to the USSR not for 'safe keeping' but to be used to buy arms. It is now known that the USSR massively overcharged the Republic for the aid sent, by manipulating exchange rates [97]. It is possible the Soviet Union did not make a profit from its transactions with the Republic, given the huge credits granted to buy more arms once the gold reserve had been used up in early 1938 – credit that was never retrieved [102]. However, this was still 'credit', and the evidence of the Soviet government exploiting the misfortune of the Republic while proclaiming its internationalist and anti-fascist principles to the world reinforces the view that its primary motivation was hardly disinterested solidarity (see pp. 68–70).

Apart from their dealings with the USSR, the loyalists were inevitably at the mercy of a great many unscrupulous international arms dealers. One previously overlooked episode of this trade was the sale of arms to the Republic by Nazi Germany through Greek intermediaries. The objective of such a singular operation, it seems, was to try to get hold of the currency generated from the conversion of a part of Spain's gold reserve. Confident the Nationalists would eventually win, these arms sales to the loyalists were not considered harmful for German foreign policy aims. Evidence available even points to the USSR being involved in the German–Greek arms trade with the Republic [95].

The attack on Madrid was a new experience for the Army of Africa; it now faced conditions reminiscent of the First World War. There was trench warfare, artillery, tanks and planes on both sides, and the Nationalists suffered heavy shelling and bombing. Franco knew his forces were limited but believed there were only three choices open to the Republic – surrender, peripheral defence, or deep defence – but that they would not, as in fact happened, opt for the third. The Nationalists also greatly under-estimated popular will to resist and even announced their victory before the city had fallen.

Madrid's defence was co-ordinated by a junta set up to substitute for the now absent government. The Republican commanders had little or no idea of the scale, disposition or readiness of the forces at their disposal. There was a shortage of rifles and ammunition and no anti-aircraft cover. The city's ability to resist relied on several inter-connected factors. What would prove unique, in contrast to the orthodox military strategy pursued by the Republic for most of the war, was the mass mobilisation of the civilian population in the city's defence. The organisation of street committees, building of defences and use of Soviet imagery recalling the defence of Petrograd [102] were all central to boosting popular resistance.

Parallel to this mobilisation was the timely arrival of the first meaningful outside aid. Troops arrived in Madrid from the rest of Spain, including a column headed by the legendary anarchist leader Buenaventura Durruti, who would soon die in confused circumstances. Foreign aid came with the arrival of Soviet military aid and the first International Brigades. The Comintern had decided to organise the Brigades in mid-September and during the course of the war around 32,000 foreign volunteers, far less than has often been claimed, passed through their ranks [123]. Although it is now known there were never more than 18,000 volunteers present in Spain at any one time, they would play an important role as shock troops in all the major battles to come. In the battle for Madrid, the arrival of these volunteers, along with Soviet planes and tanks, had a tremendous effect on morale as well as boosting the city's defence.

By early 1937, Soviet aid had stiffened Republican resistance and even reversed Nationalist air superiority for about six months. However, unlike fascist aid, Soviet deliveries were irregular; this was due partly to the difficulties of reaching Spain, but also to the changing priorities of Moscow's foreign policy. Some material was never replaced, particularly tanks and armoured vehicles. Moreover, as the war progressed, the quality of Italian and German armour and technology improved, largely in response to battlefield experience. It is calculated that in order to compete on an equal basis with German and Italian tanks, the USSR would have needed to send three times as many tanks and six times more men than it actually did [102]. The provision of tank advisors allows a good comparison to be made with the quality of German and Italian aid to the Nationalists. Soviet training personnel sent to Spain were restricted in both number and, given the acute lack of interpreters, their ability to communicate. In contrast, there were far more Italians and Germans sent to train Nationalist tank crews, with whom there were few problems of communication both because of the linguistic overlap between Spanish and Italian and because many of the Germans had some knowledge of Spanish, or, unlike their Soviet counterparts, were taught it [102, 134].

Recent research has clarified that Soviet aid compared in quantity, at least during 1937, with material sent to the Nationalists, but that the quality was very uneven. While tanks and planes tended to be the best Moscow had, the light arms provided were of diverse origin, often poor, outdated and of many different calibres thus creating endless problems in combat situations. Just over 2,000 military personnel were sent by the USSR to Spain during the war, of which no more than around 500 were present at any one time [102]. What is questionable is the extent to which the 600 or so Soviet military advisors among these personnel determined Republican strategy and organisation [78, 138, 140]. Soviet advisors, for example, were claimed to have been the architects of the Popular Army and behind the defence of Madrid. The effectiveness of this advice is unclear, however. Language problems and only brief periods of duty in Spain undermined advisors' efforts. In addition, the paranoia and fear that characterised Soviet politics at this time made it very difficult for military advisors to always make a sober and honest appraisal of each situation. Failures, for instance, were often explained as being the result of sabotage.

Despite being ordered to be tactful, Soviet reports also describe some of the advisors as 'small tyrants', and recount how 'distrust' and incompetence harmed Soviet military assistance [102, 118]. More importantly, as Daniel Kowalsky concludes, 'collaboration between Soviet advisors and Spanish military commanders was often obstructed by Moscow's desire to achieve a political programme in Spain that had little to do with military victory' [102].

Luckily for Franco, once his assault on Madrid had ground to a halt, Republican forces in Madrid were too depleted to mount a serious counter-offensive. The Nationalists were not in a position to launch a major new offensive either. In the north, Mola was too weak to take the rest of the Basque Country; in the east the front had stabilised, and in the south, the rebels were still threatened by the loyalists. The resistance in Madrid, however, had changed the nature of the conflict. It was now not a war of rapid movement, but of great battles, of tactical manoeuvres to achieve strategic objectives in which a few hundred yards of land had meaning. In this sense, clearly the First World War was the model. The Nationalists had hoped to achieve belligerent status by taking Madrid, and some thought it would mark the end to the war. Instead, it was seen as the first great international defeat for fascism and would inspire both Republican resistance and international support for what would now become a long and even bloodier conflict.

Halted at the gates of Madrid, Franco became even more dependent on foreign aid. The Germans, despite complaining about Franco's tactics and even threatening to withdraw if their advice was not accepted, now began to send not just planes but also tanks, artillery and a whole range of high-quality arms. Along with this, in December the first detachment of the German Condor Legion arrived, which subsequently amounted to some 19,000 pilots, artillerymen, military advisors, specialists and other personnel [106, 133]. Mussolini also dramatically increased his aid to the Nationalists, establishing the *Corpo di Truppe Volontarie* (CTV), fully equipped with artillery, armoured vehicles of all types and seven hundred planes. The over 80,000 troops sent by Mussolini during the war would prove crucial to Franco's military survival.

After a failed attempt to cut the Coruña road in December, the Nationalist attempt a month later to encircle the capital from the east resulted in the battle of Jarama. The rebels relied once more on the Army of Africa, and the Republicans on newly formed

Popular Army units and recently arrived International Brigade troops. Both sides suffered heavy losses. Although the battle resulted effectively in a stalemate, it meant Franco had failed to cut off the city.

Meanwhile, Nationalist forces, spearheaded by Italian CTV mobile columns eager to prove themselves, launched an offensive on Málaga. While the defence of Madrid showed the benefits of popular mobilisation, the fall of Málaga in February has been attributed to the shortcomings of the militias, and possible government negligence [57]. The city's defence was further weakened by the absence of the fleet, probably withdrawn because of both the presence of Italian submarines and Soviet pressure for it to escort ships bringing aid [51].

One result of the swift taking of Málaga was that both Franco and, even more so, Mussolini, greatly over-estimated the efficiency of Italian troops. The CTV was now used to spearhead an offensive around Guadalajara. The Italians expected to take Madrid in a lightning campaign and score a great victory for fascism. Bad weather led to the CTV motorised column getting bogged down, impeded the use of long-range artillery and prevented Italian and Nationalist planes from taking off. The lack of a promised diversionary attack at Jarama has led to speculation that Franco deliberately avoided helping the Italians so as to put an end to their attempts to undermine his military authority (see pp. 63–4). As a result of the defeat, Italian forces were now distributed in Spanish units and under Spanish command. However, to blame the débâcle on Franco's failure to keep his word, under-estimates the ferocity of Republican resistance, the role played by the weather, the poor fitness, discipline, training and morale of the Italian troops, and their commanders' mistakes. Franco's hesitancy was more likely to be the result of a desire to let the CTV wear down Republican forces around Madrid; combined with his lack of interest in rapid and sweeping victories because his own plans now centred on a war sufficiently slow to permit the thorough destruction of the enemy [51, 185]. Guadalajara was only a defensive victory for the Republicans. Yet again, the loyalist forces were incapable of following through, but the battle delayed the Republic's ultimate defeat and, above all, was a huge boost for morale.

For Franco's German military advisors the defeat around Madrid pointed to the need for a large-scale modern army and they persuaded Franco to begin mass conscription. Most importantly, Guadalajara led Franco to abandon his obsession with taking the capital, and adopt a long-term strategy. The fighting around Madrid also accelerated the process of converting Republican forces into a centralised, disciplined and, above all, politically controlled army. But the concentration of the best trained and best equipped loyalist troops in the central zone compounded the neglect of other fronts.

Total War

With the stalemate around Madrid and the consolidation of both armies, the war entered a terrible new phase in spring 1937. The variables affecting the strategic decisions of each side are disputed but most histories chart what increasingly seemed the inevitable and catastrophic defeat of the Republic. For the first time civilians experienced the rigours of what has become known as 'total war' [68, 88, 106, 137]. The population in the Republican zone was mobilised for the war effort and increasingly became the direct target of enemy bombing raids. By the end of 1937 the Republican army had become a flawed, but working entity, with around 500,000 troops. Debilitating political divisions, however, continued to undermine the Republican war effort, despite the strengthening of the state apparatus and government. The blockade imposed as a result of Non-Intervention (see p. 57) led to much transport and war material being immobilised for lack of spare parts. While the Republic concentrated its best troops and equipment for major offensives in the central zone, it lost control of the north and failed to take advantage of the relatively weak state of enemy forces on the Aragon front.

Franco now had at his disposal a militarised and politically united state, whose resources were totally subordinated to winning the war. The Nationalist army had 600,000 troops by the end of 1937, including important contingents of Moroccans and Italians. Nationalist superiority in the air and at sea was another crucial factor in Franco's favour. Unlike the Republican side, the delivery of arms to the Nationalists was not impeded by the enemy's navy or by international naval patrols. All this meant the Nationalist side could now carry out a war of attrition.

After the fall of Guipúzcoa in September 1936, the Northern zone had remained isolated from the rest of the Republic. It received little outside aid, given the activities of the Nationalist fleet, which was largely unhindered in its work as most government ships had been withdrawn to the Mediterranean. Moreover, the Republican north was beset by political problems, both internally and in relation to the central government (see pp. 89–90). The Basque 'Army of the North', was still organised along political lines, had few professional officers and lacked aircraft. Without the capacity for major offensive operations, the Basques opted for a French-inspired defensive strategy but the 'Iron Ring' built around Bilbao lacked the depth of the French Maginot Line, with which it has often been compared [54]. Worse still, one of its engineers handed the plans over to the enemy, giving yet another advantage to vastly superior rebel forces.

The northern campaign proved a useful testing ground for the German Condor Legion as it had next to no opposition in the air and Republican anti-aircraft batteries were ineffective. In particular, the strategy of air–ground co-operation, whereby planes bombed from low altitudes in support of infantry attacking fortified positions, was developed by the Condor Legion in the Northern campaign and was subsequently used to great effect by Nationalist forces during the rest of the war [106].

At the end of March 1937, the Nationalist advance began with a powerful air and artillery bombardment but achieved little at first owing to fierce resistance, the difficult mountainous terrain and bad weather. Ominously, the Nationalist high command had also decided in late March to launch its air attacks, without taking into account the civilian population. On 26 April 1937, Italian and German planes – in what would be a new departure in military terror – flattened the small Basque market town of Guernica, which, although of no military value, was a symbol of Basque national identity. The presence of foreign journalists turned the bombing of Guernica into a propaganda disaster for Franco. The Francoist version of events, which claimed that the Basques destroyed the town themselves, has long been totally discredited [196].

Meanwhile the Nationalists, in order to weaken Basque resolve, promised that there would be no reprisals, that political leaders would be allowed to be evacuated and the Basque Country would even be granted a special fiscal status in the new Spain. None of this proved true and around a thousand people were executed in the weeks following the fall of Bilbao. The Santona Pact, signed by representatives of the Basque government and the Italian forces, and ignored by Franco, was thus tantamount to unconditional surrender. Worse still, the Basque Nationalists refused to destroy industrial plant as they withdrew, leaving the region's heavy industry in the hands of the enemy. Not surprisingly, Basque separatism has been blamed for the defeat. But far more of a problem was the Republican government's lack of 'political and military flexibility', which meant it was incapable of launching effective diversionary attacks [51].

In order to take pressure off the north, Republican prime minister Largo Caballero advocated an offensive in Extremadura which could have exploited the weakness of Nationalist defences in the region. The shortcomings of the plan were that supply lines would have been stretched and troops would have been taken from the proximities of Madrid. However, it had more chance of success than an offensive in the centre (which was what eventually took place), where the Nationalists had concentrated more troops and the Condor Legion was stationed. The Extremadura plan was opposed by Soviet advisors, most probably for political reasons because it would have taken world attention away from Madrid, as well as boost the flagging credibility of a prime minister the Communists and moderate Socialists were now anxious to remove [54, 140]. Instead, in early June, an attack was made towards Segovia which held up the offensive in Vizcaya for two weeks before collapsing.

A large-scale offensive was finally launched to the south-west of Madrid on 6 July with the aim of occupying a sizable pocket of territory centring on the town of Brunete, and forcing the Nationalists on the defensive by encircling them. Masterminded by the talented chief-of-staff Vicente Rojo, it would be the first major offensive by the Republicans in the war and involved their best troops, including most of the International Brigades and 140 recently arrived Russian tanks [134]. The strategic advantage initially appeared to be on the Republican side. The zone chosen for the attack was defended by only 2,400 rebel troops and the terrain was suitable for tank warfare. The attack developed along lines that would be repeated in subsequent Republican offensives.

With the benefit of surprise and the concentration of numbers, the initial advance was the deepest and most rapid yet made by loyalist forces until it was undermined by a lack of reserves and supplies. As in similar future offensives, the Popular Army wasted time trying to overcome resolute defence by pockets of Nationalist troops instead of taking more ground, which they probably could have conquered. By not pressing home their advantage, the Republicans gave the Nationalists time to quickly bring up reinforcements. Then, in blistering heat, with no shade or water, the Popular Army was subjected to a devastating counter-attack involving massive air strikes. The Nationalist side benefited not only from being better equipped and from the more effective use of its artillery and air force but especially from the initiative shown by its middle-ranking commanders. The Republicans did manage to keep hold of two-thirds of the territory, but this meant little strategically. The offensive had perhaps only delayed the fall of Santander for another five weeks. Worse still, the Republic had lost some of its best troops and much valuable equipment at a time when its ports were blockaded [51, 54, 57]. Franco decided not to follow up his counter-offensive but to fix his positions and transfer most of his forces to finish the assault on the north. Even historians sympathetic to the rebels have argued, however, that the Nationalist command made a mistake in accepting a 'wasteful' battle of no tactical value while the vital operation in the north remained paralysed [167].

In a further attempt to relieve the pressure on Santander, the Republican army now turned its attention to Aragon, where the Nationalist army had only 29,000 troops defending a front that stretched from the Pyrenees to Teruel; although the rebels had the advantage of good communications and mobile reserves. The Aragon front had remained relatively quiet since early autumn 1936. The Republican forces in the region, which had become the Army of the East in May 1937, were mainly former militia, who had been reluctant to accept the authority of the General Staff. The lack of interest in the front and its abandonment by the central government had reinforced distrust. It has been argued that the offensive launched towards Saragossa in late August 1937, was possible because Republican authority had been established in the region (see p. 100); however, this ignores the attack on Huesca in June 1937, where, despite failing in their objectives, the former militia performed with credit.

The loss of experienced troops and material the previous month at Brunete meant this latest offensive could not be on the same scale. Within five days the Republican advance was paralysed outside the village of Belchite, which then became the objective of the offensive rather than Saragossa itself. Yet again, an initially rapid assault on enemy positions had halted around pockets of resistance. Belchite was the most bloody of a series of partially successful Republican attacks over the coming weeks, the last being at Fuentes de Ebro. Here Soviet tanks adopted the novel tactic of advancing carrying troops on top. But badly planned, this manoeuvre resulted in both men and tanks soon being isolated and destroyed [52, 134]. The Aragon offensive ended with the Republican army again incapable of taking advantage of its initial momentum, through both tactical inflexibility and limited reserves. Once more many men and much equipment were lost and, unlike at Brunete, Franco did not take the bait but decided not to halt his assault on the north, so the attack even failed in this limited objective.

On 26 August, only two days after the offensive launched in Aragon, Santander fell. It was badly defended, arms were poor, morale was low, it lacked reserves and there were very few experienced officers. Moreover, the population was tired, and divided in its loyalty. By 19 October, Asturias had fallen too. The region had become completely isolated and without provisions or war material. The Nationalists would report receiving many deserters and claim that Republican morale had collapsed. 'Mutual envy' and lack of confidence between commanders, and political rivalries, had seriously undermined the region's defence [51]. The problems facing the Republican forces in Asturias were further compounded by the absence of air and, inevitably given the government's priorities, sea support.

The victory of the Nationalists in the north was a major blow for the Republic's increasingly slim hopes of survival. The rebels had under their control for the first time a major industrial heartland. They also had thousands of prisoners, who would be used as forced labour in mines and iron foundries. The rebels' fleet could be concentrated in the Mediterranean and their troops and equipment in the centre. Franco now had sufficient forces to defend all fronts, as well as six army corps for manoeuvres, and a very structured chain of command. The victory in the north, given the prominence of Italian forces in the final offensive, also restored Mussolini's pride after Guadalajara and led him to collaborate more fully with Franco.

At an international level, the general opinion was that once the north fell it was only a matter of time before the Republic's complete defeat. To make matters worse, supplies from the USSR to the Republic had declined dramatically (see p. 91). Yet, despite the increasingly desperate situation, the Republican government did not consider altering a military strategy whose inflexibility was even more dangerous by the end of 1937 with the further increase in Nationalist air superiority. By 1937, groups of fugitives were already operating as guerrillas, but generally not in contact with the Republican command. In Asturias in particular, five months after its fall, 'furious guerrilla warfare' was reported to be taking place [54]. But the army's first and only Guerrilla Corps was not formed until after the fall of the north; it did very little, carrying out some sabotage and other actions behind enemy lines [57]. Instead, the priorities of political propaganda, for both internal and external consumption, continued to determine the necessity to carry out prestigious operations regardless of the cost.

With an expected Nationalist offensive on Madrid in mid-December 1937, a plan was drawn up by the Republican high command to divert Franco's armies by taking Teruel and the surrounding area. The Ninth Division was organised for this purpose, but many of its components were inadequately trained new recruits. In order to stress the patriotic composition of the Republican forces, it was decided the International Brigades would not be involved in the offensive. The Brigades, which amounted only to 5 per cent of the Republican military forces by the autumn of 1937, had suffered terrible losses in previous engagements; consequently morale and military effectiveness were seriously undermined. Poor leadership, inadequate training, lack of arms, and political intrigue also contributed to their debilitation. An obsession with infiltration and sabotage, and the subsequent arbitrary disciplinary measures, albeit not as extreme as some sources have suggested, added to the malaise affecting many Brigade units by late 1937 [81, 96, 118, 123].

On 14 December, the Republicans began their offensive on Teruel. Franco reacted at once, suspending the attack on Madrid and eight days later launching a counter-offensive. Senior German and Italian officers advised Franco to abandon Teruel, which had little strategic importance. But his determination to bring the Republic to a total and humiliating defeat meant he could not allow the enemy any success, even though, given the concentration of Republican forces at Teruel, he could have taken Madrid at little cost. Rebel air superiority caused havoc among the Republican recruits, some of whom would be severely punished for lack of discipline. The sub-zero temperatures added to the troops' misery on both sides, even undermining the most hardened troops, and paralysed operations. On 23 February, the Nationalists finally re-took the city after bitter fighting. Even the late use of International Brigade troops failed to stem the tide. Nationalist material superiority had again prevailed over Republican courage. The capture and defence of Teruel could be seen as a strategic victory for the Republicans because it forced Franco to stop his attack on Madrid. However, any advantage gained was countered by the appalling cost in men and material. As had happened before, the Republicans' failure to follow up its initial success reflected both the scarcity of reserves and equipment and the 'intolerable diversity' of arms. Commissars' reports point to the 'incapacity' of some commanders, and morale was further undermined by anarchist claims at Teruel of political persecution by the Communist commanders [51].

After the tremendous wasting of men and equipment at Brunete and in Aragon, followed by the loss of the north, Teruel was the military turning point in the war. More than ever, for the loyalist government, the Republic's hopes of survival depended on persuading the world's democracies to intervene, but all the courage and sacrifice caused 'not a ripple' on the international scene [153].

Franco's Victory

By early spring 1938, the situation in the Republican rearguard was becoming catastrophic. In Catalonia alone, there were now a million refugees living alongside a population of 3 million. Civilians were increasingly demoralised by hunger, successive military defeats and savage air raids. It seemed it was only a matter of time before the Nationalists were victorious, but against all the odds the loyalists held out for another year. The Republic had few options open to it other than to try to keep the war going with the hope that the expected European war would break out and lead to both the defeat of the rebels' fascist allies and direct intervention by the democracies against Franco. On the Nationalist side, the last stage of the war confirmed that Franco's aim was still to destroy as much of the Republican army as possible rather than gain a swift victory.

The Republican army was thought to be at its weakest in the east, so in March Franco launched a massive offensive along the whole Aragon front. Within six weeks much of the region had been conquered and the Republican zone was divided in two (see Map 3). In their rapid advance the Nationalists effectively used the *Blitzkrieg* tactic of massive sustained attack, for the first time – repeatedly occupying Republican positions in mountainous and easily defended country after shelling or bombing just in front of their own troops [52].

Having taken Lérida, General Juan Yagüe was for the rapid occupation of the rest of Catalonia, as were the Germans. This would have meant the definitive sealing of the French border. Instead, Franco decided to head south in the direction of Valencia through the Maestrazgo mountains. According to Francoist military historian Ramon Salas Larrazábal, the turn by Franco towards Valencia was one of the most unexpected decisions of the war. The fall of Valencia would not have been decisive either militarily or politically, while taking Barcelona would have ended the war because it would have prevented Republican forces from regrouping [167]. Franco may have taken this decision because, after the *Anschluss* (Germany's annexing of Austria), there was the possibility that the presence of Italian and German military personnel near the border might have provoked French intervention [57]. But this is unlikely to have been the real reason, given the Germans' confidence that the French were not prepared to intervene militarily [54]. Neither can the decision be reduced simply to Franco's incompetence [173]. The most reasonable explanation is that Franco seems to have thought that the sudden loss of Barcelona would still have left substantial numbers of armed Republicans in central and southern Spain [185].

Nationalist forces advanced slowly through the well defended mountainous country but when they were 50 kilometres from Valencia a new and massive attack was launched by the

Republicans across the Ebro River from the north. Apart from trying to prolong resistance until the European war began and showing the world that the Republic was still capable of fighting, the offensive aimed to avoid internal collapse at a moment when morale was at a new low.

The opening of the French border in March 1938 proved crucial to organising the new offensive. A great deal of war material, much of it of high quality, was let through but in June the border was closed again which meant that once the attack had begun the Republican army could not replenish its equipment. In contrast, the Nationalists were constantly supplied with aid during the war's biggest battle, in particular with much-needed artillery and planes. Given this context, the expressed aim to continue resistance at all costs was actually put in jeopardy by the attack on the Ebro [54].

Surprise was again on the Republican side and the advance at first was rapid. Dismayed by the Republican forces' initial success, some of the Nationalist staff advised surrounding the Army of the Ebro, which had a large river at its back, and a return to the attack on Valencia [167]. However, with constant Italian and German supplies, the French border closed and coast blockaded, Franco believed he could proceed to slowly destroy the Republican forces.

Tactically, the Republican army seemed to have learnt little from previous débâcles, and still launched a frontal attack on Gandesa rather than by-passing it [51]. Within days the Nationalists counterattacked with massive air strikes that would continue relentlessly for the coming months. Added to this was the heaviest concentration of artillery of the whole war. Despite the rocky terrain making the construction of deep defences difficult, and the overwhelming superiority of the Nationalist forces, the Republican army managed to resist. Much to the despair of the Germans and Italians, the battle went on for another four months. There was even criticism from inside the Nationalist high command, and problems with morale because of the protracted nature of the struggle. On the loyalist side, as prime minister Juan Negrín believed the whole world was watching, retreat would have been interpreted as the definitive defeat of the Republic, despite there soon being no military justification for the Republican troops to hold on [54]. It took seven Nationalist offensives and massive losses on both sides to finally dislodge the Republican forces, the last of which retreated over the Ebro on 16 November.

The Munich Conference in September 1938 (see pp. 59–60) had already been a serious blow to the Republican strategy of keeping the war going until hostilities broke out in Europe. The defeat on the Ebro left the Republic in an even more desperate situation. The Popular Army had been further weakened by the withdrawal of the International Brigades from Spain in October. By the end of 1938, the Republic still supposedly had 500,000 badly equipped men under arms but in reality this was less than 100,000 in Catalonia and barely another 100,000 in the centre. Franco's forces, in contrast, were stronger than ever. In the aftermath of Munich, the international situation was even more favourable for the rebels and Germany and Italy responded by sending yet more military hardware.

On 23 December, with overwhelming superiority, the Nationalists began their final offensive in Catalonia. A diversionary landing at Motril in the south had to be cancelled owing to the state of the Republican navy, which had been completely undermined by 'neglect, indiscipline and lack of a clear strategic and political leadership' [51]. A counter-offensive was launched in Extremadura on 5 January, but, despite the Republican army conquering the biggest area of territory at any stage of the war, it was too late to help Catalonia. The brief opening of the French border a few days later let through masses of Soviet aid, only for most of it to fall into enemy hands. Moreover, the democracies had by now tacitly accepted the Italian presence in Spain and just wanted the conflict to end, so there was no longer any possibility that the French would object to fascist forces being on their border. Barcelona fell to Franco's troops on 26 January, provoking a massive exodus of civilians towards the frontier. Internal political strife, systematic attacks on the gains made by the revolution, aerial bombardment and increasing food shortages had all combined to undermine the sprit of resistance of 1936. After final and hopeless attempts to hold up the Nationalist advance, the last Republican troops retreated into France on 13 February.

The military history of the war finished with the fall of Catalonia (see Map 4). The population was not in any state to sustain further resistance. In the centre the military authorities insisted to Negrín that resistance was impossible. The sense of complete impotence was reinforced by the abortive Casado coup in March 1939 (see pp. 103–4). By 22 March, the 'honourable peace' that Casado and others had sought had become 'unconditional surrender'. Eight days later Madrid was occupied. The remnants of the Republican army had fled to Alicante, where they waited in vain to be evacuated by a navy that had already set sail for North Africa. On the quay some committed suicide rather than surrender to the advancing Nationalists; thousands more faced captivity and an uncertain fate. The war had ended.

3 Foreign Intervention

The Democracies

The Civil War's causes were essentially internal but its outcome was largely determined by the intervention, or non-intervention, of the great powers of the time. Prior to the war, Spain had figured little in the calculations of these powers. The war would mean a diplomatic realignment of enormous importance at a critical juncture in international politics. But it also became the centre of world attention because it appeared that the great political causes of the time were being fought out in the peninsula.

The Republican war effort was totally subordinated to winning the support of the democracies. However, strategic and political preferences would mean that France and, particularly, Britain would prove impervious to appeals to intervene on behalf of the legitimate government of Spain. Instead they backed the policy of Non-Intervention – which allowed the fascist powers to aid the Nationalists unhindered.

At first the Republican government was optimistic about receiving support from the main democracies. France's Popular Front government initially was prepared to send military aid to the Republic. Apart from any ideological sympathy, the French needed to have a friendly government on their southern border and to safeguard their commercial and military routes through the western Mediterranean to their North African colonies. Some material was shipped across the frontier during the first days of the war but internal and external pressure would soon stop this. Not only did the Right threaten mayhem if the government sent aid to the loyalists but the French high command openly sympathised with the rebels. The latter argued that support for the Republic could provoke a European war which France would enter divided, without British assistance and with the armed forces unprepared [99]. Later Soviet involvement in the war confirmed the French high command's fears that the Republic represented a threat to French interests. Ironically, France reversed its policy after speculation in the press about the possibility of Italian and German intervention, while in reality Italy hesitated to send aid to Franco for fear of clashing with the French [117]. Inside the French Popular Front, the Radical Party was also uneasy about supporting the Spanish Left, especially given the influence of extremist elements in the first months of the war. Even the Socialist leaders were quite clear that any other policy than neutrality could have provoked civil war in France itself [112]. At least as decisive as domestic politics in persuading the French government not to intervene was pressure exerted by the British. It was made clear to Paris, in early August, that the French 'siding with any side' in Spain would negatively affect relations between the two governments [84].

Britain's motives for not supporting the legitimate government in Spain were two-fold: appeasement, and antipathy towards the Republic. Appeasement had its roots in fear of Communism, economic depression and an Empire challenged by Japan in the East and by Germany in Central Europe. Britain's aim was to confine the war to Spain, block French support for the Republic, prevent any move towards an Anglo-French alliance with the USSR and 'side-step' any conflict with Germany and Italy as a result of these powers' aid to Franco. In particular, the British wanted to maintain the equilibrium in the Mediterranean, both by guaranteeing Spanish good will, on which the security of Gibraltar depended, and through rapprochement with Italy. At a time when the British sphere of influence was at its most extended and there were budgetary limitations, the Royal Navy considered that it could not confront Mussolini while defending the Empire elsewhere [54]. Accordingly, throughout the Spanish war Britain would pursue the chimera of an agreement with Italy both to secure stability in the Mediterranean and in the hope that Mussolini could be prevented from moving closer to Germany. In fact, the Foreign Office did not rule out collaboration with both Italy and Germany if Spain and France were 'menaced by Bolshevism' [111]; a threat which appeared very real to the British Cabinet in 1936.

While strategic considerations were at the centre of London's decision to back Non-Intervention, even as early as 1931 the British government was hostile to the Republic, despite knowing little about what was happening in this 'far away country'. By the spring of 1936, it was aware that a military uprising was being planned. However, the British Cabinet saw Azaña as a Spanish Kerensky – who as prime minister in Russia in 1917 had been unable to hold back the revolutionary hordes. The plotters themselves assured London that they had no connection with Italy, that British concerns were not threatened and all they wanted to do was to 'restore order'. Forty per cent of foreign investment in Spain was British, but although there was concern for business interests this was not central for the government given that this only represented a very small percentage of British investment throughout the world [104, 111, 112].

Foreign Office reports on the situation in Spain accepted Nationalist propaganda about a 'Bolshevik' take-over [104]. Prime minister Stanley Baldwin's only known order to his Foreign Secretary, Anthony Eden, in relation to Spain in July 1936 was that Britain must avoid at all costs ending up fighting on the 'side of the Russians' [84], revealing both his priorities internationally and his ignorance about what was happening. At this stage, upper-class opinion did not, in general, see fascist expansion as a threat to the Empire. In contrast, the USSR was treated with universal hostility, as was the Spanish Republic, which was soon perceived to be increasingly under Communist influence. Even when the Republican government, had, by mid-1937, established its authority at the expense of the revolution, official British perceptions of what was happening in Spain hardly changed.

The reticence of the democracies to become embroiled in Spain and their desire to contain the war in the peninsula led directly to the policy of Non-Intervention. France, probably encouraged by Britain [93], took the initiative in calling for an international conference on the war in Spain. On 9 September, 27 countries agreed to the principle of Non-Intervention and a Committee (NIC) was established to oversee the policy. Among the signatories were both the fascist powers and the USSR. The agreement had taken most of August to hammer out, with Germany and Italy prevaricating while at the same time rushing arms to the Nationalists.

Rather than a serious impediment to foreign intervention, the NIC would be a toothless body aimed at extricating the democracies from any responsibilities towards the Republic. The very rules of the Non-Intervention Agreement, as Tom Buchanan explains, 'seemed designed to obstruct any investigation, through bureaucratic delay, that might offend Italy or Germany' [84]. Thus it neither avoided the internationalisation of the conflict nor dissuaded the fascist governments from an increasingly aggressive foreign policy.

The highpoint of the NIC's ephemeral activity would be the setting up, in April 1937, of naval patrols and new border inspections. From April until June 1937, French, British, German and Italian ships patrolled Spain's coasts with the right to detain merchant ships found in its ports. The aim of the patrols and port inspections was not to capture arms smugglers as such, as Italy and Germany would have never agreed to that, but to carry out inspections of ships and to denounce activity violating the Non-Intervention Agreement. The measure was too late to stop the already massive foreign intervention in the war. Britain, the driving force behind the patrols, knew, however, that they would be relatively useless [112], and they were soon abandoned after Italy and Germany withdrew following the alleged torpedo attack on the German cruiser *Leipzig*.

With the ending of the naval patrols, Franco feared more arms would reach the Republic so the Italians responded with increased submarine activity in the Mediterranean. The submarines neither identified themselves nor even ensured that the ships they attacked, many British, were travelling to Spain. This led in September to the Nyon Conference, where the British, French, Italians and Germans agreed to protect trade routes. However, these restrictions on submarine activity just led to more widespread Italian and German air strikes on boats suspecting of transporting aid to the Republic.

The general opinion in the Foreign Office was that Franco's embryonic regime was essentially different from and independent of the Italian or German regimes, and Franco himself was a decent patriot [110, 111]. Not only did government circles believe that Franco posed no threat to British interests but they looked forward to the promised stability a Nationalist government would bring and the resulting political and financial benefits for Britain [78]. In November 1937, the British Cabinet effectively recognised Franco's administration as the *de facto* government of Spain and exchanged diplomatic agents.

The war continued to be dangerous for Britain's interests however, because it divided domestic opinion and hindered efforts to separate Italy from Germany and weaken the latter's objectives in Eastern Europe. The British government was therefore no longer prepared to let the war in Spain obstruct improving relations with Italy, and saw Franco's victory as a necessary contribution to this aim [110]. Anthony Eden, in contrast, had begun to see the scale of fascist intervention in Spain as a serious threat to British interests but his resignation in early 1938 removed any internal opposition to government overtures to Italy. The resulting Anglo-Italian Treaty of April 1938 confirmed that Italy would leave Spain as soon as Franco won the war, and thus led to Britain tacitly condoning Mussolini's intervention.

Meanwhile, in France, Socialist prime minister Leon Blum's sympathies for loyalist Spain had at times led to his administration relaxing the stringencies of Non-Intervention, by turning a blind eye to volunteers and small amounts of arms crossing the border. The French had also still hoped Italy could be detached from Germany [99], but this ended, with Germany's annexation of Austria in March 1938 (the *Anschluss*). In exchange for accepting Nazi control of Austria, Germany now recognised Italian hegemony in the Mediterranean. Faced with this, and the Nationalist threat to Catalonia, Blum once again considered supporting the Republic. Nevertheless, after clashing with his chiefs-of-staff, who feared this could both provoke a general European war and alienate the British [112], he just opted to re-open the border to let through military material. This would be the only time that France took an independent line of action in relation to the war in Spain. In the meantime, despite Soviet protests and French misgivings, the NIC remained in place. A British proposal for the withdrawal of foreign troops from Spain merely helped maintain the fiction of Non-Intervention [108]. Britain believed such a withdrawal would clear the way for an armistice, which both sides would be forced to accept, so closing the French border was essential and this duly took place in June. A new French government, without Socialist participation, now looked forward, like its British counterpart, to a Franco victory.

Despite 'anti-British phobia' in the rebel press and open support for the fascist powers, Nationalist leaders were aware of the benefits of British policy [110]. When the Munich Agreement –

whereby Britain and France acquiesced in the face of Hitler's designs on Czechoslovakia – was signed in September 1938, the Nationalists reacted by informing London that Spain would remain strictly neutral in the event of any European conflict. Hence the Foreign Office's faith that the 'liberal dictator' was no threat to imperial interests was confirmed. The British government had clearly decided that Franco's victory would not pose a problem for Anglo-French *entente* because Franco would be too exhausted to participate in any future European war, his government would need finance for post-war reconstruction and Anglo-French naval power would dissuade the Nationalists from any hostile action.

With the war staggering to a close, the British government insisted that before obtaining from Franco any guarantees over reprisals or evacuation, the Republic had to announce it was prepared to surrender. On 27 February 1939, Britain unconditionally recognised Franco's government. The following day Chamberlain lied to the Commons that Franco had given an assurance there would be no reprisals against Republican prisoners [111].

In contrast to Britain and France, the other major democracy, the USA, remained at the margins of enforcing Non-Intervention. Its policy of strict neutrality was the result of both the pressure of isolationist tendencies in Congress and the aim of the State Department to achieve a system of collective security. But the US government, like Britain, had been hostile to the Republic since its foundation [105]. Many US politicians saw the Popular Front as Soviet-inspired. Moreover, President Roosevelt depended on Catholic voters, who were hostile to the anti-clerical Republic, and, when the war began, generally favourable to the Nationalists [78]. In contrast, Claude Bowers, the pro-Republican US ambassador in Madrid, was largely ignored.

On 11 August 1936, the US government declared a 'moral embargo' on selling arms to Spain. In January 1937, the 1935 Neutrality Act, forbidding the sale of arms to other countries, was extended to include civil wars and the embargo became obligatory. Yet while the US government observed strict neutrality, this was not the case with US companies, which sold thousands of trucks and over 3 million tons of oil to the Nationalists. The view in business circles was that Franco was fighting a Spanish version of the New Deal. However, during 1937, neutrality as a policy began to be undermined by public pressure. There was a massive campaign of solidarity with the Republic in the USA, which attracted the active support not only of the workers' movement but also of many prominent intellectuals and public figures. In early 1938, there was even a US-backed attempt at an international peace initiative but this came to nothing, in part, because the British did not take it seriously [90].

By the end of the war, Roosevelt, in the face of growing fascist aggression internationally, was considering intervening in Spain [129]. Roosevelt may have been involved in a plan to illegally ship 150 American aircraft to France in June 1938 to help the beleaguered Republic defend itself. Given Roosevelt's tendency to duplicity in his private statements on foreign policy, there is some doubt as to his involvement in the scheme [97]. However, at the end of the war he seems to have regretted not having intervened in some form and warned of the negative consequences of the Nationalist victory for the democracies [129].

The other democracies followed the lead of Britain and France in abandoning the Republic to its fate, as did an inept League of Nations [130]. One exception was Mexico. A few weeks after the uprising the Mexican President Lázaro Cárdenas rushed 20,000 rifles and 20 million cartridges to Spain. This is often cited as the sum total of the Mexican contribution. But although it has been impossible to quantify the amount of military aid sent, recent research shows that there were more deliveries during the course of the war [113]. Despite this inevitably being less than the Soviet contribution, Cárdenas's government still made an 'extraordinary effort' to help the Republic. Its modest arms industry was given over to aid the Loyalist cause. Mexican army officers were also sent to advise their Spanish Republican counterparts. Abroad its embassies represented democratic Spain, especially in Latin America, where most governments were hostile to the Republic [90]. Mexican diplomats acted as intermediaries to buy arms, and Republican representatives often travelled with Mexican diplomatic documents. The Mexican flag flew, as a cover, on Spanish ships transporting military aid. Finally, the Mexican government, unlike the USSR, accepted payment for these arms in pesetas, despite the peseta's increasing devaluation and Mexico's own economic problems [113].

The shared goals of the two Republics or Cárdenas's idealism have been cited as reasons behind the Mexican government's decision to send military aid to Spain, but internal considerations were

61

probably more important. The Spanish Civil War polarised domestic politics. Militant anti-clericalism and rising class conflict in Mexico made Catholic and middle-class sympathy for the Spanish Right even more relevant. Fearful that a Franco victory would encourage the Right to launch a coup, Cárdenas saw a Republican victory as tied to the defence of his left-wing programme in government and the legacy of the Mexican Revolution as a whole. Cárdenas also hoped that by insisting that the Republic had the right to defend itself he could persuade the great powers, in particular the USA, to support the Spanish government [113]. Official solidarity continued once the war finished, with the acceptance of some 30,000 Republican refugees. Mexico would stand alone in never recognising Franco's Spain.

The Fascist Powers

Fascist and Nazi intervention was central to the Nationalists' victory: an intervention that began immediately with the sending of Italian and German planes to ferry the Army of Africa over to the peninsula. Nazi Germany benefited more than any other great power from its involvement in Spain. It obtained economic advantages not only in relation to the import of raw materials but also through important military experience and the subordination of Italy to its long-term strategic aims. In contrast, Italy would gain little from what is now known to have been its massive involvement in the Spanish war [79, 94, 116, 117].

The Italian government had sponsored both monarchists and Falangists in the pre-war years, but later claims by Mussolini that he had done everything he could to overthrow the Republic cannot be substantiated. Although it has generally been accepted that Mussolini had little relationship with the military plotters, recent research shows that in June 1936, in the weeks leading up to the uprising, the Italian secret services had been in contact with them [94]. For many years it was believed that Mussolini was persuaded to intervene by the Spanish Monarchist leader Antonio Goicochea and by the fact that France was supposedly sending arms to the Republic [93], but neither was the case. In reality, Mussolini was convinced to act by secret service reports claiming that neither France nor Britain nor the USSR were going to intervene and that

Franco controlled the army, was going to win soon and would subordinate himself to Italy [94].

Despite, like Hitler, stressing the struggle against communism as his prime motive for aiding the Nationalists, strategic considerations were the chief reason for Mussolini's decision. It has long been understood that Mussolini wanted both a friendly Spain bordering his enemy France and hegemony in the Mediterranean at the expense of the democracies, especially Britain [79]. Achieving these aims would, he believed, shift the balance of power in the zone towards Italy and prepare the ground for what he was convinced would be the inevitable war between democracy and fascism. Rather than territorial or economic gain, Mussolini thus insisted on certain strategic conditions in return for aid – the most important of which was that future Spanish policy in the Mediterranean was in harmony with that of Italy [122]. Morten Heiberg has demonstrated that Mussolini's ambitions went even further: that he actually aimed at the establishment of a fascist state in Spain and its submission to Italy [94].

Mussolini was encouraged to take a bellicose stance by his newly appointed foreign minister, his son-in-law Galeazzo Ciano, who set out to give Italy a totally fascist foreign policy. Victory in Abyssinia and national resentment at the resulting League of Nations sanctions meant that Mussolini was at the height of his popularity and confidence. Convinced that a small quantity of arms would suffice for the Nationalists to win, the Italian decision to intervene was taken without any serious investigation into Franco's chances of success [116]. Apart from his strategic aims, Mussolini's pride would drag him deeper into the Spanish war at every turn. The war became a question of his personal prestige and would, he believed, end in victory not just for the Nationalists but for international fascism. Within five months, to all intents and purposes, Italy had declared war on Republican Spain.

With the failure to take Madrid, and having rashly recognised the Nationalist government, the Italians accepted Franco's requests for further aid, not only by sending more material but by organising an Italian expeditionary force, the CTV (see p. 42). Given Italy's commitment in Abyssinia, its assistance could not have been greater. However, recently published diplomatic documents show that while Mussolini insisted that Franco should be enabled to win the war, the Nationalist leader's failure to accept Italian political and military advice created serious doubts about whether aid should continue [78]. By the end of February 1937, Mussolini had even announced that no more troops would be sent. But after the Italian defeat at Guadalajara, any doubts Mussolini had were dispelled as the credibility of fascism had to be restored. The *Duce* now found himself not only more involved than ever but being forced to subordinate the command of his troops to Franco, whose conservative tactics he held in so much contempt.

Mussolini was not manipulated by the Germans into a greater commitment in Spain, as has often been claimed. Although there were several high-level meetings between Italian and German leaders to discuss joint military and political co-ordination in Spain, rather than Mussolini being forced into further commitment, it is now clear that he was an enthusiastic participant for his own imperial interests [94]. Moreover, the more the democracies showed themselves unwilling or unable to challenge Italy's blatant intervention in Spain, so Mussolini was more determined not only to continue but to increase his involvement. In case anyone had any doubts about Italy's intentions, as early as March 1937, its representatives on the NIC announced that no Italian 'volunteer' would be withdrawn until Franco's victory was complete and official. For the Germans, the benefits of Italy's heavy involvement would only become evident after Mussolini had totally committed himself to the Nationalist cause.

The German government seems to have had no knowledge of the imminence of the coup. Neither did the German Foreign and War Offices favour aiding the rebels when the uprising started. Hitler alone appears to have taken the decision to intervene, quite coincidentally, after two envoys sent by Franco – Nazi businessmen resident in Morocco – managed through personal contacts to get an audience with the *Führer* [132].

While anti-communism was a factor in this decision, broader strategic considerations played a more significant role [103, 131, 132]. As the Spanish war would show, Hitler's foreign policy, despite its clearly opportunist character, had an underlying logic in the sense that it was subordinated to the general vision he had about German power in the world. After July 1936, the Nazis aimed to avoid the forming of a hostile alliance between a victorious Republic and its Popular Front counterpart in France, which in turn could have led to a new French agreement with the Soviet

Union. As the war progressed, the economic exploitation of Spanish resources became increasingly important to Germany. A hostile Spain might have deprived Germany of vital minerals and removed an important centre for intelligence and communications [103, 131, 133].

Like Mussolini, Hitler initially believed that low-level intervention would be enough and the war would be over quickly. Once this clearly was not the case, and he felt sure that the democracies would not challenge German interests, he committed himself fully to Franco's victory. Although claiming that Spain was 'a convenient side-show' that would absorb the energies of the great powers, leaving Germany a freer hand in the East, the subsequent transformation of the war into a long and costly affair would modify Hitler's strategy in Spain. German economic interests became increasingly important as the war dragged on [103].

As payment for aid, Germany obtained desperately needed raw materials such as iron ore, pyrites, mercury and other minerals, for its rearmament programme. The state-sponsored export and import companies, HIMSA and ROWAK, set up to channel vast quantities of minerals and other raw materials to Germany, operated a virtual monopoly over trade between the two countries; private interests and conflicting concerns being 'ignored or even suppressed'. The Nazis' aim was, effectively, to transform Spain into an 'economic colony' [103]. Economics overrode any friendship treaty, thus in the summer of 1938, at the height of the battle of the Ebro, when Franco requested more aid the Fürher insisted on the need to guarantee Germany's iron ore supply. In fact, in the end it appears Hitler was in no hurry for the war in Spain to finish, so that he could continue to exploit the economic advantages to the maximum while Germany rearmed [95, 133]. Hitler also understood that his intervention in Spain would undermine Britain's ability to obtain these raw materials, especially after the fall of the Basque Country. Prior to the war Germany had imported roughly the same amount of iron ore from Spain as Britain but by 1938 this had increased three-fold.

German armour and air power and the arrival of crucial material proved decisive for Franco. Hitler's decision to send the Condor Legion (see p. 42) was in part determined by his initial disappointment with Franco's slow progress and even more so by his annoyance with the rebel leader's mistaken strategy. Franco in turn accepted that in exchange for more German aid, the Condor Legion would be led by German officers, but submitted to his command [133]. So although it is generally accepted that German military advisors at times influenced Franco, as clearly seems to have been the case, for instance, in relation to the offensives on Bilbao and Teruel, they did not determine his strategy [57]. Hitler even considered sending troops but decided not to because this might have led to the very coalition between the democracies and the USSR he was trying to avoid.

Apart from Italy and Germany, Portugal played an important role, especially in the early months, in supporting the Nationalist war effort. With the election of the Popular Front government, relations with Portugal had become strained, given its government's ties with the fascist powers and the fact that thousands of Spanish rightists took refuge there. With the first news of the uprising, the Portuguese regime offered to send troops, claiming a Republican victory would lead to a 'Soviet invasion'. The Portuguese Legion was founded in September 1936, but its around 10,000 troops were mostly absorbed into the Nationalist army and wore no distinguishing insignia so were less visible than their Italian or German counterparts. More importantly, Portugal also provided the rebels with food and credit, and became a rearguard base for the Nationalist government to bring in economic and, especially German, military aid. Republican sympathisers who fled over the border during the first weeks of the war were promptly handed back to the Nationalist authorities. At an international level Portugal was of considerable use to the rebels. In the League of Nations and in the NIC the Portuguese representatives effectively represented the Nationalists to the world, and served, when necessary, as intermediaries with France and Britain [78, 119, 125].

The Soviet Union

The nature of Soviet intervention in the Spanish war remains the subject of controversy. Despite claims that Stalin's policy aimed to achieve a Republican victory, the evidence available suggests a far more opportunist approach, solely conditioned by the strategic needs of the USSR. In particular, the search for an alliance with the democracies against Nazi Germany was an immediate priority when the Civil War started. As a consequence, Soviet policy was subordinated to this end at least until it became clear that the forming of such an alliance was increasingly unlikely. Within this framework it is possible to see the inconsistencies in Soviet policy regarding Spain as being designed to avoid a Republican defeat rather than to secure a victory.

Initially the Soviet Union had opposed sending arms to the Republic, despite prime minister José Giral's direct appeal for military aid when the rebellion started. Apart from the massive logistical problems involved in such an enterprise, Stalin was anxious not to get embroiled in a conflict that could only harm his attempts to achieve collective security. The Soviet Union's participation in the NIC, according to Geoffrey Roberts, was due to its aim to help the Republic politically if it could not do so militarily [121]. With this in mind, a solidarity campaign was launched both inside the USSR and abroad through the Communist Parties to send non-military aid. Inside the NIC, the Soviet representative Ivan Maiskii was an untiring defender of the Republic and continually denounced fascist violations of the agreement. Meanwhile, the Soviet Union had sent its first diplomatic representatives to Spain, accompanied by numerous military advisors.

Recent studies suggest that it is most likely that Stalin took the decision to send military aid in late August or early September. A plan, known as 'Operation X', was then drawn up by Military Intelligence and the secret police (NKVD) and was subsequently presented to Stalin for his approval, presumably in mid-September 1936. Although the USSR could benefit politically from supporting the Republic by presenting itself as the principal bulwark against fascism, rather than Stalin fulfilling his role as 'world revolutionary leader' [114], what most probably led him to change his mind was the extent of foreign fascist support for the Nationalist side and consequently the real possibility of imminent Republican defeat. The war in Spain put Stalin's government in a very difficult situation given its attempts to form an alliance with the Western democracies, particularly France, against Nazi Germany. Intervention could have jeopardised the building of such an alliance, but leaving the Republic defenceless would have strengthened fascist power throughout Europe. Stalin still hoped that German and Italian intervention would persuade the democracies that the fascist governments were a real danger for peace. Unavoidably, Soviet support for the Republic had two distinct, but equally negative, consequences: it deeply accentuated British and French distrust of the loyalist government and it was the ideal pretext for a qualitative and quantitative increase in aid to the Nationalist side from the fascist states.

For decades it was very difficult to ascertain the exact quantity of Soviet arms dispatched to Spain. Newly published documentation suggests that the amounts sent were less than was claimed by official Soviet sources [97]. What is accepted is the decisive role this aid played in the first year of the war in sustaining Republican resistance. This military and human support was accompanied by a great deal of propaganda and cultural material such as films and books, which was distributed by the newly opened Soviet embassy and by Communist front organisations [102]. The existence of this aspect of Soviet shipments to Spain poses an interesting question about Soviet intentions given that most other evidence suggests that Moscow did not want too much attention drawn to its involvement.

The aid sent by the USSR could not compete with that received by the rebels from the fascist powers. Most was delivered in the first ten months of the war and some deliveries were never repeated, thus leaving the Republican forces without replacement material. The Republic was never able to manufacture satisfactory tanks and planes, and was nearly totally dependent on the Soviet Union for such crucial equipment. From mid-June 1937, acts of solidarity with the Republic or even information in the press all but vanished inside the USSR. At the same time, aid declined drastically, vital spare parts were not provided, neither tanks nor planes were replaced and advisors spent too short a stay in Spain to have much effect. Consequently, some historians speak of the USSR 'abandoning' the Republic, at least from the beginning of 1938, if not before [78, 83, 140]. The slowdown in deliveries paralleled increasing discussions in the NIC about the withdrawal of foreign troops and the subsequent recognition of the belligerent status of each side. The latter would have effectively meant the end of non-intervention as both sides would have been able to search foreign ships and blockade each others' ports unhindered. However, British opposition would ensure belligerent rights, which at this stage would have clearly benefited the Nationalists, were never granted [78, 84].

Different reasons are given for the decline in Soviet aid. Lack of sufficient naval power, the costs involved in transporting aid and the problems of the Soviet military industry meant it was difficult to supply Spain for any length of time or at least with substantial quantities of material. The situation was made worse after June 1937 by limited access over the French border and the increase of Italian submarine attacks in the Mediterranean. In addition, by the summer of 1937 arms were being sent by the Soviet Union to China and Mongolia rather than Spain. Also, as recently published documents show, many Soviet personnel considered the war a lost cause. In March 1938, the gold deposited by the Republic had been used up and, although the Soviet government granted two substantial credits, to have continued sending large quantities of aid would have cost millions of dollars that it might never have recovered. Above all, the realisation that an agreement with the democracies was increasingly unlikely probably contributed to growing Soviet indifference towards Spain. The Munich crisis would prove the final nail in the coffin of collective security; the USSR was now more preoccupied with the defence of its own borders [52, 78, 102, 118].

One enigma is why, after having virtually abandoned the Republic during 1938, did Stalin agree to the request by the loyalist government to send desperately needed military supplies in December 1938 – even though this would be considerably less than was promised and some of it of a poor quality [95, 97]? A participant in the Republican delegation to the USSR has suggested its trip was successful because Stalin was unaware of how serious the situation was in Spain, owing to his personnel being afraid to tell him the truth [52]. A more convincing explanation was that it reflected the arbitrary and inefficient nature of Soviet intervention.

Stalin's policy in Spain has been seen either as responding to events as they unfolded [121]; as clearly aimed at Republican victory; or as primarily designed to sustain Republican resistance and thus avoid defeat. According to Daniel Kowalsky, Soviet leaders made a great effort to win the war but this proved 'unsustainable' so was 'prudently aborted' and thus can be considered a complete operative failure. Citing Soviet documentation, he argues, as does Tim Rees, that by sending the best equipment and personnel, issuing insistent orders for decisive action to be carried out, providing military training for thousands of Spaniards and deciding to send an important cargo of arms right at the end of the war,

Stalin demonstrated his desire for outright victory [102, 120]. For others, the desire to win a military victory cannot be separated from Soviet plans to establish a proto-Communist regime in Spain (see pp. 91–2).

The sending of high-quality military material and the training of Spanish pilots does not, in itself, prove that Stalin wanted to win the war. First, direct military advice was not always based solely on the immediate strategic and technical needs of the Republican army but reflected Soviet political aims in Spain. Secondly, while a fascist triumph was undoubtedly against Soviet interests, as it would have strengthened its enemies, a Republican victory, on the basis of strong Communist support and influence, would have probably impeded any collective security agreement. In the circumstances, the Soviet government could well have believed the only way to achieve such an alliance would be in the course of the inevitable European war, thus the aim was to sustain the Republic until the war became generalised throughout the continent [56, 140]. Moreover, as the war progressed and the chances of winning support from the democracies faded even further, the Republican government also saw that its only hope of survival was to hold out until a general European conflagration broke out. Thus if Soviet strategy was aimed principally at avoiding Republican defeat, both the decline in aid in 1937 and the last desperate attempt to prop up resistance in December 1938 can more easily be understood.

International Solidarity

The Spanish Civil War had a massive impact on domestic politics throughout the world. Political divisions, both between Left and Right and within the Left itself, intensified as a result of what was happening in Spain. The workers' organisations, which were particularly sensitive by 1936 to the dangers of fascism, instigated a massive campaign of international solidarity. Thousands of foreign volunteers went to Spain to defend the Republic, and many died. Spain became a touchstone for left-wing politics and identity for decades to come.

In the democracies hundreds of thousands of citizens were involved in different forms of solidarity with Spain. In Britain probably no other international event in which the country was not directly involved caused such a deep impression. Spain was different because it 'appeared to embody the great ideological conflicts of the day, the defence of civilised values, be they democracy or Christianity, against a barbaric enemy' [84]. Support for the Nationalist side, as elsewhere, came mainly from sectors of the upper and middle classes. The majority of Conservative MPs supported the Nationalists, as did the upper echelons of the business world and the Church hierarchy. A series of right-wing commentators, journalists and military experts trooped around the Nationalist zone providing a steady stream of pro-fascist propaganda for domestic British consumption [100]. Those Conservatives opposed to Franco were usually not sympathetic to the Republic but believed, like Winston Churchill did, that a Nationalist victory would lead to Spain becoming a client state of Italy and Germany and thus threaten British interests in the Mediterranean.

The National Government's huge majority meant activity in support of the Republic was decidedly extra-parliamentary. Public opinion gradually swung in favour of the loyalists as a result of the intervention by the fascist powers, events such as the bombing of Guernica and the continual attacks on British shipping. Among intellectuals the war in Spain had a 'cultural, even spiritual significance' [84]. Fascism was the new barbarism assaulting freedom of speech and thought. In Britain, as elsewhere, the Civil War inspired an outpouring of literature, poetry and art sympathetic to the Republican cause [65, 96, 109, 128]. By January 1939, 71 per cent of the population had declared their support for the Republic. Even 48 per cent of Conservative voters were supposedly sympathetic to the loyalists. Unfortunately there were no polls taken over Non-Intervention. However, it could be argued that much of this sympathy was passive, as support for Chamberlain and appeasement was still 'remarkably buoyant' [84].

The Labour Party and Trades Union Congress (TUC), while declaring their support for the Republic, initially backed Non-Intervention as the best way to preserve peace but insisted that it be effective [85]. In June 1937, the official labour movement abandoned this policy in the face of events and called not only for the Republic to be allowed to buy arms but also for a great campaign on behalf of Spain. But this was largely ineffective because the Labour Party and TUC were unwilling to force the Government to change its policy by extra-parliamentary means as they feared this would upset Labour's electoral chances. The movement's leadership also wanted to avoid a split inside the party and the unions over the Civil War.

In Britain, as elsewhere, the Communists were at the forefront both in organising solidarity with the Republic and in combating home-grown fascism. The Civil War gave the small British Communist Party a chance to challenge Labour's hegemony on the left. As in other countries, the turn away from its previously sectarian line meant the party broadened its support throughout society, especially among intellectuals [85, 96]. The Communists were central to what was subsequently referred to as the 'Aid Spain Movement'. Based on hundreds of ad-hoc committees, and involving many rank-and-file Labour Party and union members, it mainly organised the sending of humanitarian aid through the widespread raising of funds in streets, workplaces and local labour movement organisations. The Aid Spain Movement was strongest in urban and industrial areas, especially in London, South Wales [127] and Central Scotland. Funds were also raised for direct relief work in Spain itself and by 1939 the National Joint Committee for Spanish Relief was responsible for caring for 8,000 children in the Republican zone. The same Committee had organised the receiving and care in Britain of 4,000 Basque children in May 1937. More overtly political, and one of the most important bodies, was Spanish Medical Aid, which worked directly with the International Brigades and local hospitals in Spain. The Communists gained particular prestige from their role as organisers of the International Brigades. Some 2,300 British volunteers were sent to Spain, mostly to fight, others as medical personnel, and many prominent young party members died or were wounded [81, 96, 98].

On the Nationalist side there were few genuine foreign volunteers, one exception being the 700 or so Irish led by Eoin O'Duffy of the clerical-fascist Greenshirt movement. As they hardly took part in the fighting, most accounts are dismissive of the Irish fascist volunteers. Their relevance lies more in the context of the support provided for Franco by Ireland's all-powerful Catholic Church [126]. There were also, in the ranks of the Foreign Legion, up to 500 French-speaking volunteers and small groups of White Russians and Romanians [100].

The around 32,000 volunteers that fought with the International

Brigades came from at least 53 countries. The volunteers were recruited through the Communist Parties, with the French party playing a central role in co-ordinating the operation. On 22 October, the Republican government formally accepted the establishment of the Brigades, within which all foreigners fighting with Republican forces would supposedly be integrated. Independently of the Brigades, up to 2,000 international volunteers fought with the CNT militia and several hundred more with the POUM.

Few of the Republic's international volunteers had military experience; most had been activists in their own country, often involved in street fighting against fascists. A significant proportion of volunteers were refugees from authoritarian governments. Memoirs and literary works have given the impression that intellectuals were prominent in the Brigades, but the reality was that around 80 per cent of volunteers were of working-class origin, among which 'worker intellectuals' were well represented. Most were young and single. Jews were disproportionately represented, reflecting the important role they had in anti-fascist struggles in Europe at the time [81, 86, 96, 123].

The Brigades were not 'Communist' organisations as such, and the presence of non-Communists seems to confirm their 'Popular Frontist' character [81, 153]. However, evidence of Communist control is fairly overwhelming. Well over half the volunteers were party members and it was the Comintern that decided both the setting up and the dissolution of the Brigades. Most importantly, over 500 foreigners resident in the USSR and members of the Soviet Communist Party were sent to Spain. Many had served in the Red Army, some during the Russian Civil War, and now became officers and commissars in the International Brigades. They were particularly prominent on the Brigades' General Staff [123]. The majority of the remaining officers were members of their respective Communist Parties. Given the central role of the Communists as organisers and inspirers of the Brigades, their pre-eminence at all levels is hardly surprising. Moreover, Communists dominated the Brigades' internal security services. An unknown number were members of the NKVD who were also active in the Republican zone as a whole, in particular in investigating, and sometimes intervening against, foreign dissident communists.

The International Brigades were an important focus for solidarity abroad and served as a supposed example of the Popular Front in action. When former volunteers returned to their countries of origin, they were often prominent in raising support for the Republic [84, 86, 96]. The fact that the volunteers had been relatively isolated from the Spanish population, and not directly exposed to the complexities of Republican politics, helped perpetuate the Communist view of the war. Fear of adverse propaganda abroad and sensitive to accusations of foreign Communist involvement in Spain, the Comintern agreed in December 1936 that the Brigades' role should not be exaggerated or contrasted too favourably with that of Spanish troops [118]. By the summer of 1937, although the Brigades continued to intervene in all the major actions of the war until their withdrawal in late 1938, they more or less disappeared from Republican propaganda, reflecting the increasing importance of the Popular Army as much as the need to downplay foreign intervention.

The fate of volunteers who came from countries with dictatorial regimes, when the Civil War ended, was particularly dramatic. In the summer of 1939, it was reported that the majority of the 6,000 Brigade members in French concentration camps were Communists from countries where their party operated clandestinely. Many of those who did manage to survive in France ended up in the Resistance; others died in Nazi death camps. The 1939 non-aggression pact even meant some German volunteers who reached the USSR were handed over to the Nazis. Even those foreign Communists who had been sent from the USSR in the first place were not guaranteed to return. Some former volunteers would be among victims of purges in the post-war Communist regimes; others, in contrast, became leading figures in these same regimes. Above all, the memory of the Brigades would take on legendary proportions for the Left, internationally, for decades to come as one of the most heroic symbols of anti-fascism.

Prelude to World War?

The Spanish Civil War, Non-Intervention and intervention had an impact on the subsequent fortunes of the world powers. Non-Intervention failed to appease the dictators. Intervention hardly benefited Italy and the Soviet Union. Only Germany really gained an advantage, both economically and militarily, from its participation in the Spanish war. Above all, the Civil War can be seen as a rehearsal for, or at least a prelude to, the Second World War.

The ideological fault lines of the coming conflagration were present during the Civil War. It also signalled the arrival of a terrible new form of modern warfare. In terms of the actual origins of the Second World War, historians have generally given more importance to events in Austria, Abyssinia and the Sudetenland than in Spain. Yet, as Willard Frank argues, on the road to world war, the confrontations created by ideology, rearmament, Abyssinia and the Rhineland crisis were channelled through Spain, and while the Civil War was not a direct cause of the eventual conflagration it did speed up the European crisis [91]. Most significantly, the Spanish conflict clarified the question of when European governments would or would not be willing to go to war. A delineation of the contending great power blocs was thus one of the clearest results of the Civil War.

The weaknesses of the democracies were neatly exposed by their refusal to intervene in Spain. According to Mary Habeck, the Spanish war prevented Franco-British unity against the dictators in that it distracted attention from far greater dangers [93]. Thus while the French General Staff were convinced that Non-Intervention had stopped the conflict from spreading and hence France had avoided war with Germany, Soviet involvement in Spain led France's military establishment to cling to the erroneous strategy of trying to resurrect the military agreement with Italy. Moreover, the French army's sympathy for the Nationalists was not reciprocated once the Civil War finished, and instead of an ally France found itself with a hostile neighbour [99].

Britain's policy of compromise, rather than calming the international situation, only heightened tension between the European powers. The British government failed to understand that Spain was another arena where Germany and Italy were testing how far their aggressive stance could be taken. In fact, both Italy and Germany were concerned at the beginning of the Civil War that Britain would make Non-Intervention effective. The one time that the British government did take a tough line against flagrant violations of the Non-Intervention Agreement, over Italian submarine activity in the Mediterranean, showed that a stronger policy against the fascist powers' involvement in Spain would not have provoked the European war Chamberlain feared [79]. Neither did the British

General Staff prove capable of learning any military lessons from the Civil War [87, 88]. Finally, the lack of involvement of the USA in Spain, even in Non-Intervention, pushed it still further away from the European democracies [91].

The Civil War also alienated the Soviet Union from the West. Receiving no response to appeals for collective security, Stalin became increasingly convinced that appeasement would channel Hitler's attention towards the East. As early as December 1937, coinciding with the effective paralysing of Soviet arms deliveries to Spain, Stalin indicated his interest in rapprochement with Germany. By the last weeks of the war, he appeared to have dropped any attempt to align with the West. However, even at this stage, Stalin did not completely abandon the Republic – as the last-minute sending of aid seems to show – or rule out altogether an alliance with the democracies. In April 1939 he would launch his most ambitious plan yet to secure a collective security agreement, with the attempted negotiations with Britain and France for a Triple Alliance. However, Soviet suspicion that the democracies would opt for another version of Non-Intervention and leave the USSR isolated led to the negotiations' failure [121]. At a more sinister level, given subsequent events, the Spanish war also established the precedent for Soviet intervention in the internal affairs of other countries. Finally, the USSR benefited little from the military experience to be gained in Spain. Soviet military leaders were afraid, or incapable, of breaking with conservative military orthodoxy for fear of being identified with their more capable colleagues who had recently been purged from the ranks. Thus the Soviet Union neither kept up with the extremely fast development of fighter design, as Germany did, nor did it adopt and develop techniques of co-ordinated air–ground attacks on enemy infantry positions. Equally short-sighted was the Soviet high command's rejection of the independent use of tanks after being faced in Spain with the effectiveness of German anti-tank weapons [52, 134].

The consequences for Italy of its intervention in the Civil War were nearly all negative. Defeat in the Second World War was blamed by many Italian fascist leaders on the loss of vital material in Spain. Stanley Payne, however, claims that the material lost in Spain made little impact on Italy's subsequent military effectiveness because it was old equipment that needed replacing and military spending had actually dropped between 1937 and 1938. The real sources of Italian weakness in the Second World War, he concludes, were deficient leadership and organisation, an inadequate industrial base and a failure to develop advanced weaponry [115]. Recent research, in contrast, confirms that the wastage of equipment in the Civil War did indeed damage Italy's subsequent war effort [117]. The immediate costs in resources, and constraints on Mussolini's freedom of action, meant his victory in Spain was decidedly hollow.

Neither did Mussolini's aim to impose Italian-style fascism on Spain after Franco's victory succeed; and nor did Spain become a faithful ally, as he had assumed. Instead, Spain remained neutral in the coming European war and, worse still, became a potential rival to Italy for France's colonial possessions in North Africa. In the end, Franco's grandiose ambitions were similar to the *Duce*'s: to be the emperor of a re-born nation, to dominate the Mediterranean and to conquer the old French empire [94].

By intervening in the Civil War, Italy also mortgaged any agreement with Britain and became tied irredeemably to Germany, although the long-term benefits for Hitler were not immediately apparent [91, 117]. The negotiations with Britain over the status quo in the Mediterranean in 1937 and 1938 have been presented as showing that the alliance that would take Italy and Germany into the Second World War could still have been avoided [55]. Finally, Mussolini had also hoped that, through national mobilisation, victory in Spain would achieve the internal stabilisation of the fascist system. However, the duration of the war, with few spectacular victories and high losses, led to a sensation of exhaustion and disappointment which, combined with the growing fear of war with France and Britain, finally undermined support for the regime [55].

Hitler emerged as the principal beneficiary from the manoeuvring of the five great powers over Spain because it proved a convenient place for him to make diplomatic, economic, propaganda and military experiments [133]. On an economic level, the raw materials gained by Germany helped rearmament. Although Goering's attempt to turn Spain into an 'economic colony of Germany' failed, the German state import company ROWAK continued to play a central role in the economic relationship between the two countries until 1945 [103].

Militarily, rather than just test out preconceived tactics, as has often been claimed, Germany accrued invaluable lessons from its combat experience in Spain, which it would put to use in the early part of the next war. The air war, in particular, had a 'tremendous impact on Luftwaffe combat doctrines' [106]. Unlike the democracies or the Italians, the Germans learnt from the disaster at Guadalajara in that it showed how the new technique of *Blitzkrieg* required absolute command of the air and an abundant supply of tracked vehicles, not merely a preponderance of armour. The Condor Legion perfected concentrated low-level attacks to support infantry in advancing and occupying enemy positions, and the effective use of the new Messerschmitt Bf 109 in the later stages of the Civil War proved a rehearsal for the Battle of Britain [54, 72]. In other ways the conditions in Spain mostly did not prefigure those of the coming world war [51]. Strategic bombing, for instance, apart from some devastating examples such as Guernica, Barcelona and Lérida, was not such a significant aspect of the war owing to the technical limitations of the aircraft available [52, 106]. Finally, the war in Spain demonstrated to the Germans the best tactical use of maybe the most efficient of all Second World War ground weapons, the 88mm anti-tank and anti-aircraft guns [106].

More importantly, the appeasement policies pursued in the western Mediterranean by the democracies finally convinced Hitler that his plans for territorial expansion could continue without recourse to war. According to Frank, Hitler was thus testing something more important than arms in Spain: 'British mettle'. During the course of the Civil War, Hitler's attitude to Britain turned from 'esteem to scorn'. His policy of expanding 'with or without Britain' became one of 'against Britain'. After Austria, Hitler moved into Czechoslovakia confident that neither Italy nor the democracies would oppose him. In fact, if it were not for the lessons he learned in Spain, Frank concludes, Hitler would not have gone to war so soon [91].

4 Politics and Society in the Republican Zone

Social Revolution

Popular resistance did not lead just to a Civil War, but to the disintegration of the Republican state and the beginnings of a far-reaching social revolution in much of loyalist territory [56, 62, 138, 140, 142, 148, 164, 165]. The revolution expressed itself in a multitude of ways: from the ever-present armed workers, rapidly organised into militia columns, through to the organisation of daily life, supplies and security, the changes in women's lives and, especially, the collectivisation of sectors of the economy. Although this multifarious revolution appeared largely spontaneous, the long-term aspirations of the workers' movement, both anarchist and Marxist, provided the context for this sudden transformation. The collapse of the state, in particular its monopoly of armed force, made this possible. The revolution gave an impulse to the resistance to the military uprising that the Republican authorities alone could never have inspired.

The Republican government, its institutions and its army nominally continued to exist but their authority or capacity to act independently was seriously undermined. To speak strictly of 'dual power' however, is misleading, as there was no alternative base of power as there had been in Russia in 1917, the obvious parallel [147]. Instead, power in the Republican zone was now fragmented into countless anti-fascist committees and militias, many a world unto themselves [56 138, 140]. These committees were usually established by the different workers' organisations and reflected the strength of any particular group in a given locality. Others were Popular Front committees and included representatives of the

Republican parties. In most areas regionally based committees attempted to co-ordinate both armed resistance and the organisation of the rearguard. The most important of these were the Anti-Fascist Militia Committee in Catalonia, the Popular Executive Committee in Valencia and similar bodies in Asturias and Murcia.

The depth and nature of the revolutionary movement generally reflected the pre-war strengths of any particular faction in the workers' movement. So Catalonia, with the largest concentration of industry, and the traditional stronghold of the CNT, became the centre of the revolution, along with rural eastern Aragon. In Valencia, the influence of both the CNT and the left Socialists also meant that the urban centres and parts of the countryside were initially under the sway of the more radical elements. In Madrid, despite its being effectively under the control of the workers' organisations, the proximity of the front, the long-standing influence of the Socialists and the important presence of the Communists meant the social revolution was hardly felt. In Andalusia, the revolutionary process was also conditioned both by the front and by the loss of important centres like Seville and Córdoba. Isolated from the central zone, the social revolution in Asturias was not as wide-ranging as in the east, but the workers' movement dominated the region.

Widespread repression throughout the Republican zone was one of the most immediate popular responses to the military uprising. In the first weeks there was little co-ordination or control of rearguard security, which had passed into the hands of the workers' organisations, usually in conjunction with the Assault Guards. Extensive and precise local studies over recent years demonstrate that around 38,000 people were executed in the Republican zone during the war, about half in the first six weeks of the war [64]. The choice of victims was not arbitrary [143]. Targets for popular anger included not only rebel army officers, rightist leaders, landowners and other members of the ruling classes but also rank-and-file members of reactionary parties, unpopular foremen, Civil Guards or members of Catholic unions. Shopkeepers, foremen and managers with a good reputation were generally spared.

Terror in the Republican rearguard has often been blamed on so-called 'uncontrollables' and the anarchists – the dividing line between the two being blurred for some observers. In particular, the 'uncontrollables' were held responsible for revenge killings and robbery and are usually depicted as common criminals, many freed at the outbreak of the war. As for the anarchists, they were not alone in spreading terror. Repression was just as widespread in areas where the CNT hardly existed [18, 171].

In contrast to the rebel zone, in Republican-held territory both the authorities and all the political organisations, including the CNT, sought to end arbitrary killings as soon as they could. Unlike rebel leaders, many Socialist and Republican leaders were appalled by the blood-letting and tried to protect those seized. Repression in the Republican zone was neither 'profitable' nor had a 'specific social function' as it did in the opposing zone [188]. It contributed very little to the aims of the Republican government and was soon brought under control, with new forms of popular justice being introduced by local and regional powers. There were still cases of unauthorised killing; the most notorious being the massacre of 2000 fascist prisoners near Madrid in November 1936.

Given the greater freedom enjoyed by journalists in the Republican zone, reports about repression in the rearguard were far more frequent in the foreign press than from the Nationalist side and were very damaging to the loyalist cause. Nationalist propaganda, which exaggerated and distorted the nature and extent of killings in the Republican zone [145, 187, 196], was faithfully repeated by the conservative press outside of Spain and has seen a revival in present-day 'revisionist' accounts of the war [67, 68]. The more lurid descriptions of Republican repression, especially the savage abuse of clerical victims [146, 171], are still usually based on unreliable Francoist sources. Despite the sweeping repression that followed the war, those responsible for this abuse were never found, it usually being blamed on the enraged 'mob' [64]. This alone should serve to undermine the reiterative accounts of anti-clerical sadism.

The first weeks of the war saw an unprecedented assault on the Church and its servants. Up to 7,000 clergy lost their lives. The persecution did not distinguish between orders: those involved in charity and social work were just as likely to be victims as those most closely connected with the ruling elites [187]. The burning of churches, effigies and other religious artefacts, often in a clinically organised way, reflected both popular rejection of organised religion and the more or less spontaneous desire, particularly among the anarchists, to purge the old world while creating the new.

Usually the 'reallocation' of churches and other religious buildings was 'eminently rational' and they were converted into garages, warehouses or meeting halls [148, 159].

Conservative accounts have tended to present anti-clerical violence as the continuation of persecution, during the Republic and before, by liberals, freemasons and other radical tendencies. Likewise, murdered clergy are portrayed as passive victims in these accounts [33, 146]. Recent studies point to contributory factors such as male resentment of priests' control over women, or popular rejection of priests' sexuality as not 'normal' [14, 31]. The abundance of 'counter-rituals', inspired by religious ritual itself, especially popular ritualised violence, was another contributing factor. This violence, however, must be located in the context of the Church's role in actively supporting the existing order, for which it provided ideological justification [29, 34, 171, 174]. The persecution was thus not so much anti-religious, as against the Catholic Church as an institution.

Where the revolution in the Republican zone went furthest was in the economic sphere with the collectivisation of agriculture, industry and services. The nature of this process differed from region to region and had few precedents prior to the war. Most collectives had an extremely practical aim: to keep production and services functioning, to adapt to the specific conditions of war and to get the harvest in, to feed both the front and the rearguard [138, 142].

The main centre of urban collectivisation was Catalonia, where 40 per cent of both industry and services were expropriated; in Barcelona this rose to nearly 80 per cent. Most firms were taken over spontaneously in the first days of the military uprising before the CNT issued instructions to its members to do so. The idea that workers should and could run the economy for the benefit of society as a whole had permeated sections of the working class over the years through cultural associations (*Ateneos*), co-operatives, unions and written propaganda [20, 144]. For the CNT, whose militants provided the backbone of the revolution, collectivisation was a means to an end: the socialisation of economic production. Its unions, at a local and regional level, therefore drew up plans over the coming months to establish the basis of the new economy [164].

Collectivised firms were run by factory councils, involving both blue and white collar representatives and in a few cases the former employer. These councils were elected by mass meetings or based on existing union bodies. Even when elected they tended to consist of established union leaders and activists. There were also sub-committees dealing with different aspects of running the collective. Although independent union committees were supposed to guarantee workers' conditions, in practice they did not always carry out this role given the involvement of the unions in the management of the collectives. The level of participation of the workforce in taking decisions on running the collective differed from workplace to workplace. At a city and region-wide level, many industries were formed into associations to co-ordinate production.

In most collectives there were moves towards reducing wage differentials. Nurseries were sometimes established, reflecting the integration of women into industry. Training and education was also organised and work was occasionally given to those previously involved in 'pernicious activities', such as 'prostitutes, gamblers and boxers'. Yet with production being subordinated to war aims and the need to enforce work discipline, not surprisingly some workers became as alienated from the 'new' economy as they had been from the 'old' [168]. Given the context of war, shortages of raw materials and the disruption of trade and transport, many urban collectives were surprisingly efficient. In some cases, industrial plant and stock was in a better condition when it was returned to its owners at the end of the war than when it had been taken over [138].

Where the collectivisation process went furthest was on the land. By 1937, there were some 1,500 different rural collectives involving one and half million people [142]. Most of the land collectivised had belonged to large landowners or fascist sympathisers or was taken over on the basis of the voluntary merging of existing small-holdings. While in some cases collectivisation was enforced from outside, in most the peasants and farm labourers themselves took the initiative.

Formally the CNT recognised the rights of small property owners to continue cultivating on an individual basis but in practice some were obliged to work collectively. Whether peasants rejected or supported the collectivisation process tended to depend on their class interests, the poor and landless understandably being the most enthusiastic. In Valencia, for instance, collectivisation was backed by poorer peasants, sharecroppers and labourers but fiercely

83

opposed by conservative smallholders [141]. In Aragon, the Catalan anarchist militia played an important part in spreading collectivisation, with local Socialists and Communists generally opposed to it. In Castile and Andalusia, in contrast, the UGT had a leading role in the process [142]. Catalonia was a case apart; most peasants were reluctant to give up individual cultivation, and collectivisation took place mainly where sharecroppers or tenants were poorer.

Most agrarian collectives were run by an elected committee, and they brought under common use such things as fertilisers, seeds and machinery. In many rural collectives, artisans and traders also took part. New schools and cultural centres were often established and literacy campaigns launched. The most radical experiments in collectivisation took place in eastern Aragon and reflected both the poverty of most villages and the fact that the state had collapsed altogether in this region. A system of vouchers often replaced money. This was not necessarily for ideological reasons, as has often been assumed, but because the absence of the state and the subsistence nature of the local economy made the use of currency unnecessary. The distribution of goods and food took place on the basis of villagers' needs. Any surplus produced was re-invested in the collective. For those embracing libertarian ideals there was a strong ethical undercurrent to the collectivisation process in the 'sharing of poverty', which was as important as practical economics. Women, however, participated little in the running of the collectives and even received a lower minimum wage than men, illustrating the limitations of egalitarianism, even in revolutionary Aragon [138, 142].

The co-ordination of agrarian collectives, especially during the first year of the war, was usually undertaken by the rural unions, which drew up plans to improve and organise collective production. The most ambitious of these regional organisations was in Valencia, where the CNT arranged the exporting of citrus fruit on a massive scale [141]. In Aragon, the Council of Aragon co-ordinated production, consumption and exports [28, 142]. It has been difficult to ascertain to what extent the agrarian collectives were effective but, taking into account the adverse circumstances in which they operated, most evidence suggests that agricultural output was more or less sustained.

Everyday life was also profoundly affected by the situation

created by war. Recent studies reinforce contemporary eyewitness accounts of the visual impact of revolutionary Spain, especially in Barcelona. In some of the poorest neighbourhoods there was a pre-war culture of resistance and occupation of urban space and this provided the basis for the embryonic process of social transformation now beginning in different cities in the Republican zone [20, 148, 166, 190]. As a consequence there was an increase in social services, such as new hospitals, and the common use of occupied property. Hotels and exclusive restaurants were expropriated and communal eating houses provided a vital service for the civilian population. In Catalonia, public services were generally expanded and eventually brought under municipal control.

Many women had their lives transformed by the social revolution, despite gender roles remaining basically intact [152, 162]. In the rear, women played a decisive role in maintaining civil resistance by working in social services, nurseries, collective canteens and child care, as medical volunteers and providing assistance to refugees [162]. As in most modern wars, women were integrated into the workplaces to replace men at the front [6]. But in contrast to other wartime experiences, women in Spain were often working in industries that had been collectivised, or at least were under some form of workers' control.

One important area of mobilisation was through left-wing women's organisations. The very public role of certain women – especially the anarchist minister Frederica Montseny, the Communist leader Dolores Ibárruri and the Socialist deputy and intellectual Margarita Nelken – challenged, however partially, traditional male dominance of politics [38, 39, 161, 162]. The most important women's organisation was the Communist-led Anti-fascist Women's Association (*Agrupación de Mujeres Antifascistas*, AMA), which mainly mobilised women in a supportive role to the men at the front and in favour of the Popular Front. The libertarian *Mujeres Libres* (Free Women) was an exception in that it had a fairly independent existence and insisted on women's liberation as an end in itself rather than just a by-product of proletarian revolution. While demanding the incorporation of women into the work-force, *Mujeres Libres* gave more importance to education. Its continuing assertion of its autonomy meant that it never received the sort of funding that the Libertarian Youth received or that the Spanish Communist Party provided for the AMA [135, 150].

The participation of women in the militias has been one of the most potent images of the revolution, presenting what appeared to be a dramatic rupture with the past. However, the few women that went to the front often found themselves confined to traditional female roles such as nursing and cooking. All Republican organisations, without exception, soon advocated the sending of women not involved in such ancillary tasks to the rearguard. Very few continued in the front line [156, 162].

As the war progressed and the revolution declined so Republican propaganda emphasised women's role as mothers and wives, even though 'anti-fascist' ones. Even *Mujeres Libres* organised women to carry out typical gender-based tasks such as sewing clothes for the militia, working in the hospitals and raising funds for the families of the fallen or for refugees. Attempts by *Mujeres Libres* to eradicate prostitution met with limited success [135]. That women did not manage to break decisively with their subordinate role reflects the limitations of both the revolution and the workers' movement. Women were also heavily influenced by their previous experience of gender roles and did not necessarily accept situations that transgressed these. Nevertheless, seen within the context of 1930s Spain, the new collective dimension to women's role in public challenged traditional female passivity and this was a liberating experience, leading women to acquire a new self-respect and confidence, awareness of their rights, and more control over their own lives [162].

One area where women played a particularly active part, in the loyalist zone, was in the spreading of education and culture. Belief in the 'redeeming' role of culture, so prevalent among Republican reformers in the pre-war years, remained as strong during the war. The Republic actively promoted the use of culture to mobilise the population against fascism [24, 136, 166]. In particular, education reform, far from being abandoned in wartime conditions, continued apace. Literacy campaigns were organised at the front by the Culture Militias (*Milicias de la Cultura*) and in the rear through the activities of the Flying Brigades (*Brigadas Volantes*). Thousands of schools were constructed during the war itself. Radical teaching methods, particularly those advocated by the libertarian-influenced Free School (*Escuela Libre*), became even more widespread [11].

Cinema and theatre blossomed in wartime conditions. The Republican authorities and organisations saw the advantages of using these mediums to educate, and not just to entertain. Soviet influence was also particularly evident, especially during the siege of Madrid, with the widespread showing of Russian revolutionary films and the use of agitprop theatre to raise morale [24, 102, 158]. However, rather than develop an alternative 'revolutionary culture', bourgeois culture was 'democratised'. In Barcelona, the CNT collectivised the theatres and cinemas, but in general traditional plays and commercial films continued to be put on. The main activity of the libertarians was directed towards written propaganda and making documentary films aimed at boosting morale [24, 148].

With the printing houses expropriated by the anti-fascist organisations, there was also a massive increase in the number of newspapers published both weekly and daily, locally and nationally. Specialist papers of all kinds were produced, at the front, for women, or on cultural matters. Radio stations were also taken over and the Spanish war was the first where the radio played an important propaganda role. The graphic arts were marshalled for both popular entertainment and political propaganda. Despite the unmistakable Soviet influence, 'capitalist' design remained evident, in part due to the many former commercial artists and newspaper cartoonists involved in producing such material [157]. Intellectuals, most of whom were sympathetic to the Republic, were very active both in promoting popular culture and in attempting to rally international support [65, 128].

Rebuilding the State

Once the military rebellion had failed in most of the country and a full-scale war had begun, the divisions that plagued the Left during the Republic now returned with a vengeance, undermining a united response to the military uprising. Although this is often presented as a debate between war and revolution, in reality the dividing line, or lines, in the Republican zone were over how the war should be fought. The apparent abandonment by the CNT of anarchist principles and the spectacular growth of the Communist Party would provide the context within which the revolution would be soon sacrificed in favour of both an orthodox military strategy and the rebuilding of a liberal bourgeois state.

All factions agreed on the urgent need for political and, above all, military co-ordination. For the Republican parties, moderate Socialists and Communists, this meant the formation of a strong Popular Front government and a regular army. It also meant the 'postponement' or eradication of a revolution that they saw as hindering a unified response to the rebels and, above all, alienating both the middle classes and the foreign democracies. For the left Republicans and moderate Socialists the strengthening of the Popular Front government and the defence of bourgeois democracy was a continuation of the reformist project that they had pursued since 1931. The Communists' support for the democratic option was more complex. The PCE, following the Comintern's Popular Front line, defended the need for a broad anti-fascist front, including sectors of the middle classes, to defend democracy. In the context of Spain this policy was conditioned by war and by popular revolution. The problem was that the coup had, in Helen Graham's words, 'destroyed the fragile anti-oligarchic Popular Front alliance of urban and rural workers with middle class sectors' [153]. For the Communists this alliance now had to be rebuilt; the question was how.

For the CNT and the POUM, it was only possible to win the war by harnessing the popular enthusiasm generated by the revolution. The problem was that the anarcho-syndicalists had no strategy for pursuing the revolution beyond their practical daily involvement in the militias, the collectives, the occupation of urban space or the making of general propaganda. For most of the CNT's cadre the revolution had already been won, not only was it unnecessary to take power, but to try to do so would have only led to the establishment of a dictatorship. The POUM had a clearer programmatic conception of how the revolution should proceed but did not have the strength to carry this through. It was alone in seeing the need for a new 'class power' as the only alternative to rebuilding the Republican state [62, 137, 147].

The left Republicans had proved incapable of providing the necessary leadership either to achieve a united war effort or to re-establish the state's authority. The first step towards reversing this situation was the forming of a new government headed by Largo Caballero on 4 September 1936, which included Republicans, Socialists, Communists and Basque Nationalists. Largo was perhaps the only leader who could regain the confidence of a working class committed to pursuing social revolution and alienated from the Republican government after successive military defeats. For those forces opposed to the revolution, Largo was not a threat, despite his radical rhetoric, as he did not have a clear political strategy beyond a vague idea of anti-fascist unity through a 'Popular Front under proletarian hegemony' [53]. His government's most important achievement was to establish a unified General Staff and the creation of the Popular Army. However, curbing the revolution and achieving a truly united war effort depended on the collaboration of the CNT.

Faced with the need both for a united military response to the rebellion and to avoid its own isolation, the CNT had advocated the setting up of a National Council based on itself and the UGT but keeping Azaña as President, so as 'not to frighten foreign governments'. Once this proposal was rejected by Largo and with Madrid threatened by Franco, the CNT, claiming that circumstances had changed the nature of the Spanish state, accepted collaboration in government as necessary to win the war and protect the conquests of the revolution [139]. In early November four anarcho-syndicalists entered the government. With the authority gained by the participation of both the CNT and the left Socialists and through its control of the armed forces, credit, trade and communications, the central government could begin to re-establish the power of the state. Within months, collaboration in rebuilding the state's authority would lead to internal divisions from which the CNT would never recover.

One problem that the new unified government did not manage to overcome was the military and political isolation of the north, which developed fairly independently from the rest of the Republican zone. The Basque provinces differed from the rest of Republican-controlled territory in that there was no revolutionary movement and that a middle-class Catholic party, the PNV, was the dominant political force. As a consequence there was no take-over of industry or the land, the Church continued to function and priests even blessed Basque Nationalist troops. The Popular Front parties, despite friction with the PNV, also helped maintain Republican legality.

The PNV would have liked to keep neutral but Franco's fierce centralism forced it to take sides. Even so, the party's militias were largely passive during the first weeks of the war and in Álava and Navarre sections of its membership joined the rebel army. Only when the Madrid government granted Regional Autonomy, in October 1936, did the PNV firmly commit itself to the Republican cause. During the following nine months, Vizcaya, the only Basque territory not in rebel hands, was effectively a sovereign state with its own money, army, frontiers and foreign policy. The singularity of the PNV eventually harmed the Republican war effort, despite the heroism of its troops. When Bilbao fell in June 1937, the Basque Nationalists refused to destroy industrial installations and, as they had already tried in 1936, tried to broker a separate peace with the rebel army (see p. 46). Despite this treachery, there was no rupture between the PNV and the Republican government, in part because the Popular Front parties wanted to avoid any further divisions and the continued nominal presence of the Basque Nationalists in the central government was potentially useful to attract the Western democracies [70].

At the centre of rebuilding the state, unifying the military effort and opposing the 'excesses' of the revolution was the Communist Party, whose membership grew spectacularly in the first year of the war. Its control of what were soon mass organisations, the JSU and AMA, and its progressive take-over of the UGT were all evidence of its new-found influence. Communist growth was due to a variety of inter-related factors. By championing the Popular Front, the party obviously won credibility among sectors of the population but this was a complex relationship. Most sources claim that the major- ity of new recruits were middle class, attracted by the party's moderation and defence of order and the Popular Front [56, 140]. The term 'middle class' needs nuancing in this context, as it often includes white collar workers, whose economic situation differed little from that of industrial workers but who often felt themselves estranged from the proletariat and its organisations. However, these same white-collar sectors had shown themselves to be just as susceptible to mass mobilisation and radical politics as their anarcho-syndicalist counterparts in industry [16, 17].

The PCE attracted loyal officers through its defence of discipline and military efficiency. In particular, the party's role in the defence of Madrid and the organisation of the Fifth Regiment strengthened greatly its image as the 'party of war'. Communist control of the Agriculture Ministry helped win the party peasant support through its opposition to most collectivisation, its defence of small property holders, the establishment of producer co-operatives and the nationalisation of large estates. Helen Graham concludes that the PCE managed to deliver the 'counter-hegemonic inter-class alliance the Republicans and Socialists had sought' since 1931 [153]. If this was the case it was more by luck than judgement. The Popular Front strategy was applied by all Communist Parties, regardless of local circumstances. Moreover, one year into the war the Comintern was still bemoaning the PCE leadership's low political level [102].

The prestige of the USSR, as the only country sending substantial aid to the Republic, was also fundamental to the PCE's appeal. The fact that government censorship forbade criticism of 'friendly powers' meant that the political conditions that came with Soviet aid, or that the Republic was paying huge amounts of money for it, were generally unknown [114]. However, the attraction of the Soviet Union can be seen in a different light. What is generally overlooked in assessing Communist growth is the image of the PCE as the party of the Russian Revolution and that the Popular Front was seen, by at least some rank-and-file Communists, as a tactical interlude on the road to proletarian dictatorship [62, 123].

The reality of the revolutionary transformations taking place in much of the Republican zone presented the Communists with a dilemma. To simply declare that social revolution was not on the agenda was not sufficient to maintain popular enthusiasm. Instead, the PCE described the process underway as a 'democratic revolution' that aimed at installing an 'advanced democracy of a new kind'; 'a genuine people's democracy' as the Comintern described it. For the Communists this new form of democracy would differ from other bourgeois democracies, in that it would be based on all the Left and carry out an explicitly progressive programme that would benefit the working masses and the 'people' in general. Resuscitating the Bolsheviks' pre-1917 formula, it would be a 'special form of the democratic dictatorship of the working class and peasantry' [89, 114, 118].

The Communist position is seen by some historians as clear proof that Stalin aimed to establish a totalitarian state in Spain. Reports from Soviet personnel arguing that the Communists should take over, references to the Republic being a 'democracy of a new type' or active Communist involvement in the repression of political opponents are all given as evidence of this aim to set up a regime similar to the Peoples' Democracies installed in Eastern

Europe after the Second World War [54, 89, 114, 118, 140]. Apart from the geo-strategic context of post-war Europe in the 1940s being substantially different from Spain in 1936, Stalin's continual efforts to establish a collective security pact with the democracies would have been seriously undermined by the creation of a proto-Communist regime in Spain. Advice given by the Soviet leader and the Comintern to the PCE for most of the war suggests that such a pact remained the overwhelming priority. Likewise, the inconsistent nature of Soviet military assistance, and its sudden decline after mid-1937, hardly point to a clear strategy for a complete Communist 'take-over'. Concepts such as a 'new' form of democracy based solely on the anti-fascist parties or, increasingly, a 'national revolutionary war' had more to do with the context within which the war effort had to be forged: one of mass mobilisation and political radicalism.

The effect of Communist strategy on the Republic's war effort and rearguard was another question altogether. Verbal acrobatics alone would not overcome the divisions in the Republican camp. Instead there was a real danger that the conflicting perceptions of what was being fought for could seriously undermine the war effort.

The May Crisis

The establishment of the Largo Caballero government in November 1936 and the pressures of war itself had forced a level of unity in practice but the underlying divisions remained. In May 1937 street fighting broke out in Barcelona between the defenders and opponents of Republican order. As a consequence, part of the revolutionary Left would be suppressed and the Republican state's authority was definitively reasserted. The Communists played a decisive role in this process by providing the liberals and reformists the discipline and organisation needed to both rebuild the state and combat the revolution.

In late 1936, the revolution was still powerful in Valencia, eastern Aragon and, especially, Catalonia where the anarcho-syndicalists were strongest. The precedent to CNT governmental participation in Madrid had been in Catalonia, where in October a united Generalitat Council, including all the anti-fascist organisations, had been formed. Its establishment meant the disbanding of the Central Committee of Anti-Fascist Militias, which until then had been the real power in the region. Although the revolutionary organisations had not formed a majority of the Militia Committee, in the context of the first months of the war in Catalonia they had dominated it politically. The creation of the Generalitat Council represented a personal triumph for the Catalan President Lluis Companys. Already in the first days of revolution Companys had convinced the anarcho-syndicalist leaders that he was not an obstacle to the revolution continuing. The ambiguous image of his party, the ERC, and its mass base made it a lot easier for the Catalan Republicans than for their Spanish counterparts to reassure the revolutionaries they were not a threat [170].

The new Catalan government had a Popular Front majority, but the CNT, because of its support in the streets, at the front and in the workplaces, remained powerful. The POUM also participated in the Generalitat Council, having failed to persuade the CNT to 'take power' through the Militia Committee. The first measures of the united regional government effectively 'legalised' the revolution. Its Collectivisation Decree represented a compromise between the different factions in the government and put an end to spontaneous collectivisation in Catalonia [144]. A system of Popular Tribunals was established to try suspected supporters of the rebels. Legislation regulating civil marriage and a very liberal divorce law were introduced. Abortion was legalised and birth control made available. In education progressive methods were promoted and an ambitious programme of school building began. Such measures reflected the socio-political situation in the region. But the majority of the Catalan government, like its counterpart in Madrid, was set on a course that would limit, if not finish with, the revolutionary process. The conversion of local anti-fascist committees into Municipal Councils was a clear example of this. While beforehand these committees had often been dominated by the revolutionaries, the ERC now returned to power at a local level accompanied by the newly formed PSUC. The new Catalan administration also established a unified police force, within which no party or union membership was allowed.

The underlying tension between those who advocated continuing with the revolution and those who saw it as an impediment to winning the war was most dramatically reflected in the growing conflict between the PSUC and the POUM. The Catalan

Communists' new-found strength was in the UGT, whose ranks had swelled once obligatory unionisation of all workers was introduced. This growth was particularly marked among the white collar sectors and technicians, which provided a counter-weight to the anarchists in the collectives. The PSUC, like the PCE elsewhere, also received support from sections of the lower middle classes and peasants frightened by the excesses of the revolution. However, as with the PCE, its political base was contradictory. The PSUC's founding programme was explicitly revolutionary in tone and despite the social democratic and Catalanist origins of part of its leadership the new party was a section of the Comintern and behaved as such [16].

The virulent campaign waged by the Communists against the POUM has been put down to pre-war divisions in the labour movement or the POUM's own 'provocative' line [89, 120, 153]. However, prior to the war the forerunners of both the PSUC and POUM had shared a similar social base and, despite their rivalry, had collaborated in a series of united-front initiatives [17]. What changed the situation in 1936 was not just the revolution but also the influence of Soviet anti-Trotskyism. Already in April 1936 – and not months after the war had started, as is often claimed – the Comintern had called for the stepping up of the struggle against 'Trotskyism' in Spain [89] and as a consequence the POUM had been subjected to verbal abuse and even physical assault in the weeks leading up to the war [16]. The POUM enraged the Communists, not just because it berated them for their reformism and dismissed the Popular Front as class collaboration, but because of its very public defence of the Bolshevik leaders being executed in the USSR. The POUM's disagreements with Trotsky [147] were immaterial, as all communists perceived as dissident were denounced by the Comintern as 'Trotskyists' and by extension 'fascists'. Also the POUM was an easier target for repression than the far stronger CNT. The fact that much of the CNT leadership saw the conflict between the PCE/PSUC and POUM as a 'family' dispute and not about the survival of the revolution facilitated the dissident communists' persecution. The POUM in Madrid had already been effectively illegalised by the city's Defence Junta in autumn 1936 and in December its representative, Andreu Nin, was expelled from the Catalan government. While the Communists and their Popular Front allies did not need much encouragement to eliminate their revolutionary critics, in both cases Soviet representatives had been pressurising for this to happen [102, 118].

In early 1937, the PSUC stepped up its campaign against the 'excesses' of the revolution, which it blamed for the calamities befalling the civilian population and the thousands of refugees that had flocked to the region. In particular, it agitated around the growing food shortages with the slogan 'more food, less committees' [170]. Party leader Joan Comorera, as the Generalitat's minister of supplies, disbanded the supply committees, which had controlled distribution, replacing them with price controls. The CNT and POUM, in turn, blamed food shortages on increasing economic control by the state at the expense of the revolution. Attempts by the Republican authorities to gain control in the economic sphere were accompanied by moves to create a state monopoly over security. In Barcelona the police attempted to disarm the CNT-dominated Control Patrols, which operated against enemy sympathisers in the rearguard. By spring 1937, violent clashes between rival factions and between the police and radicalised workers had become increasingly frequent. Continual accusations in the Communist press that the POUM and other 'uncontrollables' were 'fascist agents', or fake reports about fraternisation on the Aragon front, provided further justification for attacks on the extreme Left.

Attempts to reassert Republican authority solely by administrative means and propaganda were not sufficient. Apart from the POUM, many anarcho-syndicalists still believed that they were fighting not to defend the Republic but to advance the social revolution. This unsustainable situation came to a head on 3 May, when Republican Assault Guards tried to seize the telephone exchange, a symbol of workers' control in Barcelona. The resulting street fighting proved to be a watershed for the revolution. Resistance was organised by the CNT defence committees, which, rooted in the poorer neighbourhoods of the city, had always been a base for the more radical anarchists [20]. Elsewhere in Catalonia there were clashes when police stormed CNT and POUM offices.

The POUM, whose militants joined the anarchists on the barricades, did not aim to 'conquer power' [89], but believed that the uprising had to be used to protect the gains of the revolution [62, 147]. More importantly, the POUM had, since the beginning of the war, defended the need for unity with the CNT and hence felt obliged to participate in the struggle, especially as pre-war relations with the anarcho-syndicalists had been conflictive [16, 17, 19]. But the CNT and FAI (*Federación Anarquista Ibérica*) leaderships baulked at a POUM proposal to take over the city completely, fearing any such initiative might aggravate the situation further. The calls by the anarchist ministers Juan García Oliver and Frederica Montseny for a ceasefire led to both the dismantling of the barricades and a deepening of opposition to collaboration inside the CNT. The aftermath of fighting saw widespread repression of the radical Left [149] and it would never re-gain the influence it had enjoyed in the first months of the war. The events of May 1937 have been presented as part of the process of re-establishing the authority of the state [153], or as an important step on the road to consolidating Communist domination in the Republican zone [114, 140].

The clashes in May were preceded by a virulent campaign in the Communist press, both locally and internationally, against the 'Trotsky-fascists' of the POUM. This raises the question of how far the Soviet Union intervened politically in the Republican zone and what the effects were of this intervention. Some scholars have argued strongly that Soviet interference at least determined Republican policy, if not its defeat [56, 114, 140]. More recent studies insist on the absence of any clear intention by the Soviet government to dominate the Republic [153] or at least its incapacity to control events in Spain even if it had wanted to [120]. However, even taking into account long-term inter-organisational conflict as a central cause of political strife during the war, there is considerable evidence of Soviet attempts to influence Republican politics. The Soviet consul in Barcelona, Antonov-Ovseenko, linked the POUM being expelled from the Generalitat to the sending of Soviet aid to Catalonia. Ambassador Marcel Rosenberg visited Largo every day accompanied by military and civilian personnel and his interventions went much further than just his famous clash with the prime minister at the end of January 1937. Military advisors frequently went beyond their brief (see p. 42), and there is evidence that Communist units had priority when it came to the distribution of Soviet arms [54]. Different sources also relate the influence Comintern delegates had over the PCE leadership [89, 140]. Even Daniel Kowalsky, who stresses the contradictory and ineffective nature of Moscow's intervention in Spain, concludes that Soviet 'diplomats, advisors and NKVD agents' had a 'decisive role in the design of the Republic's politics' [102].

Assessing the scale of NKVD activity is difficult given the lack of credible documentation, combined with the influence of anti-Communist and Francoist accounts which have greatly exaggerated its importance. On the basis of the documentation available, it appears that only twenty to forty NKVD agents were sent to Spain [102]. Nevertheless, given that many agents would have operated under other guises, for instance in the International Brigades, ascertaining the number of operatives present in Spain is extremely problematic. They were involved both in espionage and, more ominously, in 'finding and eradicating' the same enemies as in the USSR. The NKVD in Spain trained others to 'fight sabotage', and in May 1937 claimed it had already prepared 200 agents, who had 'unmasked a great number of dangerous organisations'. One could assume that this refers principally to the increasingly active Nationalist spy and sabotage networks [181] but, given Stalinist demonology, it undoubtedly included leftist radicals.

Kowalsky concludes that the activities of NKVD agents were probably limited to certain moments and places rather than consisting of a generalised intervention throughout the Republican zone, and that a campaign of Stalinist terror in Spain was never a priority for the Soviet authorities [102]. Any assessment of these agents' role, however, cannot ignore the context of Stalinist methods and policy at the time. Available documentation shows clearly the atmosphere of paranoia and fear that Soviet personnel operated in; not to have reported the activity of saboteurs and 'Trotskyists' would have been deemed reason for suspicion [118]. An appreciation of what was happening in the USSR itself at this time therefore is essential when trying to evaluate Soviet activities in Spain.

While it is quite possible that the Soviet Union did not directly provoke the May events [153], its foreign policy clearly coincided with the aims of the Republican parties and moderate Socialists in finishing with the revolution. Only the Communists had the organisational ability and political credibility, as a 'revolutionary' party, to carry this out. Stalinist methods and politics were thus grafted onto existing divisions and provided the backdrop to the Republican counter-revolution. In this sense, Stalinism played a central role in finishing with the social revolution underway in the Republican zone and in deepening the divisions inside the Left. The bitterness and demoralisation caused by this in-fighting could only undermine Republican resistance.

The Negrín Government: Survival or Defeat?

With the revolution crushed, Negrín's government set about both re-enforcing the war effort and consolidating governmental auhority. Within this context, the Communist Party became the dominant political force in the Republican zone and Negrín's main ally. Continual and costly defeats at the front combined with increasing hardships and aerial bombardments in the rear to undermine the newly strengthened Republican state. Final defeat would be accompanied by further violent division inside the loyalist ranks.

The removal of Largo as prime minister in May 1937 was orchestrated by his moderate Socialist rivals, who wanted someone who could 'deal with international diplomacy and encapsulated liberal democratic principles' [120, 153]. The Communists turned against Largo principally because of his handling of the war, particularly after the fall of Málaga [54, 118], rather than his opposition to Socialist–Communist unity as has been claimed [140]. More importantly, Largo had served his purpose in neutralising the influence of radical elements. The new government was headed by a moderate Socialist, Juan Negrín, and no longer included the party's left or the CNT. It would be the first truly Popular Front government, as it included the main left-wing parties and was no longer dominated by the unions [27]. Negrín's prime objective was the lifting of Non-Intervention, strengthening Republican military resistance at the front and eliminating the 'excesses' in the rear, which he believed had harmed the Republic's prospects of obtaining military aid from the democracies.

One of the consequences of the removal of Largo was the illegalisation of the POUM, blamed for the May events, and the arrest of its leadership. The abduction and subsequent murder of party leader Andreu Nin caused an international scandal that damaged attempts at projecting an image of a democratic non-Communist government. Nin had spent nine years in the USSR (1921–30), where he had become a Trotskyist, although he was never Trotsky's secretary as most sources claim. All available evidence suggests the murder of Nin was the work of Soviet agents who had hoped to force a confession from him and mount a Moscow-style show trial of the POUM leadership. As well as Nin, various other, mainly foreign, revolutionaries were murdered or disappeared.

In late June 1937, Special Tribunals were set up to investigate espionage and treason. However, their work appears to have been directed as much at the extreme Left as at fascist subversion [138]. Foreign leftists were particularly vulnerable; their cases often deliberately being mixed up with those of alleged fascist agents in order to sustain the idea of a 'fascist–Trotskyist plot'. Nearly 4,000 antifascists are known to have been imprisoned in Catalonia up until the end of the war. Most were CNT members [149]. In August 1937 a new military information service, the *Servicio de Inteligencia Militar* (SIM), was created which aimed to root out Nationalist subversion and leftist dissidents alike. The predominance of Communists in the SIM has been cited as either proof of the party's aim to control internal security [114], or reflecting the preferences of 'old' police for the PCE and PSUC [153]. It is also usually assumed that the NKVD's activities overlapped with those of the SIM [54, 140]. Private prisons, named *Checas* after the security forces of revolutionary Russia, had already been established by different organisations, especially the Communists. These were now mostly taken over by the SIM. The precise number of these prisons, or how many people went through them, is not known. There is, however, evidence that in both private and state interrogation centres fascist and anti-fascist prisoners alike were often illegally detained and tortured, or even disappeared altogether, but years of wildly exaggerated Francoist historiography has clouded the true dimension and nature of the Republican prison system.

For some historians, Republican security measures can only be understood in the context of increasingly harsh wartime conditions. Moreover, many of these measures were no different from those taken by other democracies during the Second World War and were often ineffectual [89, 153]. While a state of war was not declared in the Republican zone until January 1939, the Nationalists had imposed one from the start. Likewise, a contradictory impression emerges of the work of the Special Tribunals, which 'imposed harsh sentences', but then appear to have been lenient as many of those convicted were subsequently released [149]. This apparent benevolence, if not inefficiency, is presented as further proof that the Communists never managed to impose complete control in the Republican zone. As is the fact the POUM leadership were condemned in November 1938 to long prison sentences for having revolted against the Republic, rather than being shot as traitors as the Communists demanded [89, 120, 153].

99

But this overlooks both the impact of the international campaign of solidarity with the POUM and the fact that those most directly responsible for the May events were not brought to trial. The need of the Soviet government to placate democratic governments abroad also explains why the methods of the Moscow trials could never be fully implemented in Republican Spain.

The new government continued to employ a strategy towards the CNT aimed at incorporating part of its leadership while isolating and repressing the more radical elements. Despite the CNT initially denouncing Negrín's government as counter-revolutionary, it soon accepted the need for renewed governmental collaboration. The abandonment of anarchist ideals was such that by July 1937 the FAI was in the process of converting itself into a proto-political party [9, 143]. Opposition inside the CNT ranks to collaboration came in particular from the Friends of Durruti group, which had its roots in the influential pre-war defence committees and the militias. Although rather ephemeral organisationally, the support it received among a layer of activists, particularly in Barcelona, makes this group of interest when considering the development of the anar-cho-syndicalist movement during the later stages of the war. Its call, during the May events, for the creating of revolutionary juntas based on the CNT, FAI and POUM, which should 'take power', set it apart from traditional anarchist apoliticism. However, despite being expelled from the CNT, the group remained committed to changing the orientation of the unions rather than forming an independent organisation, let alone aligning itself with the POUM or the diminutive Trotskyist group, the Bolshevik-Leninists, as has often been claimed [147, 154].

For the government, with the POUM outlawed and the Friends of Durruti in semi-clandestinity, the only remaining focus of dissent remained the anarchist-dominated Council of Aragon. The decision to dissolve the Council on 11 August has been presented as resulting from the need to activate the Aragon front, but it cannot be separated from the on-going imposition of Republican authority at all levels. The CNT was expelled from power in the majority of villages. Land was given back to former owners and hundreds of anarcho-syndicalists were imprisoned, accused of corruption and abuse of power. The dismantling of the collectives had such a negative effect on local agriculture that many were later re-established [138].

In the economy, the new government was even more interventionist than its predecessor, aiming to maximise foreign exchange and to establish a central government monopoly of the development of key economic resources. This was 'not a politically neutral agenda'. Negrín was, as Helen Graham puts it, 'seeking to re-establish an orthodox capitalist economic order in Republican Spain' [153]. It was hoped that such measures would help convince Britain and France that loyalist Spain was striving to behave like a normal liberal democracy despite the strictures of war. Peasants opposed to collectivisation who had lost land were encouraged to reclaim it. In industry many collectives became, effectively, nationalised state-run companies, control being taken away from the workers' committees [144]. Owners were urged to return to take charge of their property but few seem to have taken up the offer.

With the strengthening of the state and the demise of the revolution, the Communists became even more central to the Republican war effort despite having only two ministers in government. Communist authority was under-scored by dependence on Soviet aid. The PCE, PSUC and JSU had accrued a massive influence inside the army and the security forces. At Brunete, Teruel and the Ebro command was in the hands of party members. Inside the UGT, the Communists, in alliance with both Socialists sympathetic to their line and Prieto's faction, had displaced the followers of Largo Caballero, who was now completely marginalised from politics in the Republican zone [151].

PCE propaganda, now virtually unchallenged, increasingly referred to the Civil War as a 'war of national independence'. Frequent references were made to the war of independence against the French at the beginning of the nineteenth century. The logic of the Popular Front was now taken further, in that the war was not 'civil' at all, but a war against foreign invaders supported by a minority of traitors. The implication of this policy was that the vast majority of Spaniards, regardless of their ideology, should stand together as patriots to defeat the external threat to their freedom. The elimination of most vestiges of the revolution of 1936 made this orientation much more feasible. The aim was two-fold: to convince the democracies of the patriotic and democratic nature of the Republic and to satisfy these same powers that Stalin had no designs on Spain.

By early 1938, Prieto, now minister of defence, had entered into conflict with his erstwhile Communist allies. In April 1938, follow-ing the fall of Aragon and the division of the Republic in two, he resigned and played no further part in Republican politics while the war lasted. According to his memoirs he had become increasing bitter about Communist proselytism in the army and the interfer-ence of Soviet advisors. Prieto's resignation, however, was due not just to his clashes with the Communists, but also to his profound pessimism and conviction that victory was no longer possible [38].

In contrast to Prieto, Negrín has been considered to have been manipulated by, if not sympathetic to, the Communists [54, 114, 140]. There was certainly a clear coincidence of aims, especially in the policy of unyielding military resistance advocated by both the PCE and Negrín. However in other questions, such as opposition to the revolution and the need to project the Republic as a 'normal democracy', he shared common ground with all the Popular Front parties. Negrín's close collaboration with the Communists can be seen principally as the result of a common war strategy. According to Helen Graham, the PCE offered Negrín 'a dynamic instrument through which to achieve the necessary psychological mobilisation of the population' [153]. However, while it is quite feasible that Negrín was not specifically sympathetic to the Communists, his orientation coincided closely with theirs and, unlike Prieto for instance, he chose to ignore the PCE's less acceptable methods. Soviet sources certainly indicate that the Communists themselves considered Negrín a close ally [89, 102, 118].

The image of the government, although damaged by the loss of Prieto, was strengthened by the return of the CNT in April 1938. The crushing defeat in Aragon had convinced the CNT more than ever that collaboration was the only option. Its abandonment of anarchist principles was epitomised by the manifesto signed with the UGT, which recognised the role of the state in economic ques-tions and the need to subordinate everything to winning the war. The CNT's pragmatism even led to it adopting a 'nationalist' discourse similar to that of the Popular Front parties [69].

Given the massive odds stacked up against the Republic by the summer of 1938, if not before, Negrín did not believe outright victory was possible. Along with the PCE, he advocated a policy of all-out resistance, with the hope that the European war would break out sooner rather than later. Negrín was convinced that France and Britain would then recognise that the survival of the Republic was in their interests. This policy of intransigent resistance and defence of a democratic and liberal Republic was symbolised by Negrín's 13-point programme launched in May 1938. This called for national unity and reconciliation, basic political and property rights, and neutrality, while subjecting Spain's future political system to a referendum. The military expression of this new determination was the massive offensive launched across the Ebro in July.

The signing of the Munich Agreement, followed by the defeat on the Ebro, really spelt the end for Negrín's policy of resistance. After Munich, professional officers questioned the justification for continuing fighting because it was clearer than ever that the democracies would never support the Republic. An exhausted and demoralised population and army was hardly in a position to continue [169], but the alternative was unconditional surrender with all that meant in terms of retribution and unbridled terror. In October 1938, the assembled remaining Cortes deputies gave Negrín a vote of confidence. This vote at least demonstrated that no one else was prepared to take responsibility for the war, and the absence of any alternative strategy by this stage. Complete pessimism now gripped most Republican leaders, no more so than Azaña, who had long since stopped playing any real role in political life. As early as November 1936, Azaña had explored the possibility of a negotiated peace and after the collapse of Aragon in April 1938 had even proposed surrender. Even Negrín did not rule out an agreement with the Nationalists and he pursued secret diplomacy for peace during the last six months of the war. But his efforts only confirmed that Franco would accept nothing less than unconditional surrender. By early 1939, with the fall of Catalonia, Negrín's position was reduced to hanging on to get a guarantee of no reprisals.

The final episode of the Republic's war was now played out in the centre (see Map 4), when, on 5 March, Colonel Segismundo Casado led a coup, backed by sections of the PSOE, the CNT and some left Republicans, against Communist forces in Madrid. Behind the coup was the emergence in the last months of the war of a renewed opposition to Communist influence in the Republican zone. The PCE's role in opposing the revolution had left a legacy of bitterness among sectors of the working class; but this opposition now went beyond the revolutionary Left to other sectors which, in practice at least, had previously accepted Communist policy. As the 'party of war', the PCE was now seen as an obstacle to peace by sections of the middle class. Communist ascendancy, in the army especially, had also led to resentment. The fact that many professional officers who had joined the PCE were passive during the Casado coup or even turned on the party demonstrates the fragility of their conversion to communism. The very size of the party was now a threat to its survival as many 'new' Communists could not be trusted. Finally, for an exhausted population and army, discipline and repression were most closely associated with the Communists [153].

Casado later justified his coup by claiming, falsely, that Communists were to be appointed as the main commanders of the army and to take complete control of the Republican zone. But neither was the PCE powerful enough to act on its own and abolish the, by now, fiction of the Popular Front, nor, as Soviet documentation shows, was Stalin interested in a Communist coup [89]. What is more likely is that Casado, who had had relations with the enemy for months beforehand, made his move to avoid his and other defeatist officers' removal by Negrín. The coup was accompanied by a forlorn and naïve attempt to achieve a negotiated peace with Franco. Socialist leader Julian Besteiro, who presided over Casado's junta, seems to have believed that Franco's regime would be like Primo de Rivera's and that by handing over the PCE, the other Republican forces could somehow purify themselves [38]. The bankruptcy of Casado's plan was 'brutally exposed' [71] as troops all along the line surrendered or just went home.

The entrance into Madrid of CNT-led troops on 12 March led to a ceasefire after eight days of fighting which had left thousands dead. This last bloody episode of internal strife, seemingly between those that wanted to surrender and those who did not, would poison relations among the Republic's former supporters in exile for years to come.

5 Politics and Society in the Nationalist Zone

The Politics of Terror

With a third of the peninsula under their control in the immediate aftermath of the uprising, the rebels began to lay the basis for their state. The heterogeneous ideological make-up of the rebels and their backers meant that a certain amount of pragmatism would be involved in the formation of the emergent regime. What became known as 'Francoism' was based on a series of upper-class and institutional interests, which to a certain extent were played off against each other to maintain Franco's control over the new state. The ideology of the Nationalist regime would reflect this heterogeneous base and would be an amalgam of fascist corporatism and religious obscurantism. Behind its ideological peculiarities would be a very clear overall aim – to eradicate all vestiges of the Republican experiment and maximise economic exploitation. In order to achieve these aims, the social base of the 'other' Spain had to be physically exterminated or, at least, neutralised through unbridled and systematic terror.

Nationalist repression was not, in general, a reaction to killings by Republican sympathisers, as was claimed at the time. Indeed, Nationalist terror was just as harsh in places where there had been no violence against the Right in the days before the rebels took control. Nor was this repression just spontaneous, as the term *paseo* (stroll), used to describe extra-judicial killing, suggests. In contrast to what happened in the Republican zone, it was systematic, organised from above and a constant factor both during the war and in the immediate post-war period [64, 175].

By extrapolating from local studies, it is possible to estimate that

105

probably around 100,000 people were executed by the Nationalists during the war and tens of thousands more afterwards. Exact figures are impossible to know as the Nationalists tended not to register deaths or at least not to enter the real cause. In fact, specific orders were given not to issue death certificates. Even if deaths were recorded, official registers were sometimes later destroyed. Between 50 and 70 per cent of those murdered by the Nationalists during the war are thought to have died between July and September 1936. Executions continued, especially in those areas where survivors were active in sabotage or guerrilla activity, until the end of the war when the repression would intensify once more at all levels [64, 175, 180, 188].

Nationalist repression also included everyday harassment and victimisation of those identified as 'red' [176]. An indication that terror for its own sake was as important as the physical elimination of those accused of harbouring dangerous ideas was that when known leftists could not be found, often members of their families became victims. The confiscation of property of Republican sympathisers was widespread and totally arbitrary. Families of those executed or imprisoned could easily lose all their means of making a living. In particular, women were held responsible for the wayward behaviour of their husbands or sons. Wives and widows of Republicans, apart from losing their property, had their heads shaved and were publicly degraded whether they had been politically active or not. As even military documents show, the rape of 'red' women was fairly common, particularly at the hands of colonial troops [80, 107]. Women also accounted for about 10 per cent of those executed by the Nationalists.

Thousands of citizens who had never played a leading role in pre-war agitation were murdered solely on the basis of denunciation by a neighbour. Personal settling of accounts, often between families, also occurred. Apart from the Falangist and Carlist militia, there was no shortage of volunteers to participate in the extermination of the 'Godless'. Particularly in the south, 'outraged by workers' demands, revolutionary threats and agrarian reform', landowners' sons, along with their retainers and foremen, were active in carrying out 'cleansing' (*limpieza*), as it was referred to. They were aided by 'common ruffians' and thugs, often from poor backgrounds, who always had been at the service of the well-to-do classes [64]. Widespread terror also served the purpose of binding together those who carried it out, as there would now be no turning back.

The terror was worse where there had been a history of struggle, and of resistance to the employers and their allies. The targets of repression were varied, not only left-wing activists and political representatives, but, as in the case of Seville, most workers as a class. Various rebel leaders advocated the extermination of the proletariat as a sanitary precaution; only economic *realpolitik* prevented this from happening. Even the Italians and Germans criticised such blanket repression as 'short-sighted' and suggested the Nationalists should recruit workers to a fascist party instead of slaughtering them [185]. The killing was so extensive in the south that there would later be a serious lack of manpower available to work on the land or in the factories. Military commanders subsequently had to adjust the level of terror to meet the needs of local employers in rural areas. The decline in the number executed in the Nationalist zone during 1937 has also been attributed to the fact that there was simply no one relevant left to kill [64].

In the early months very few victims of Nationalist repression had a summary trial before being shot, and nearly all were buried in unmarked common graves, usually by the roadside where they had been executed. Any form of juridical procedure, let alone legal guarantees for the victim, was by-passed. The law, such as it was, became a 'political weapon, a simple instrument of terror and the death penalty a general preventive measure' [175]. Even after a system of summary trials had been established there were still more people dying as a result of *sacas* (forced removal from jail) or *paseos* than from court sentences.

The wide-ranging nature of Nationalist terror was not coincidental, a by-product of civil war, but reflected a much deeper ideological outlook that sought to purge the 'anti-Spain' and eliminate the cancer of 'communism'. It had its precedents in the longer-term programme of the extreme Right [175, 180]. The rebel leaders were looking to the future. As in Germany and Italy, the aim was to terrorise and eliminate groups that did not accept the extreme Right's vision of the fatherland and to eradicate all traces of left-wing thought and activity. Most of those killed were young, between 19 and 40 years old, reflecting the Nationalists' determination to obliterate a whole generation of political activists.

Physical elimination and repression at all levels was accompanied by an ideological justification which conjured up a racist depiction of the Republic's supporters not only as 'alien' and not really 'Spanish' but also as 'sub-human', thus not candidates for Christian charity or mercy [188]. Pseudo-scientific theories were developed to explain the essentially perverse and inferior nature of the 'reds'. 'Marxism' in Spain was the product of 'foreign organic material' such as Jewish or Moorish blood. In Málaga experiments were even carried out on women prisoners to demonstrate the 'bio-psychical roots of Marxism' [189]. There were attempts to develop a theory of eugenics of *Hispanidad*, which sought to show the relation between genetics and Hispanic values. A form of 'anti-science', propounded by the Professor of Psychiatry Antonio Vallejo-Nágera, claimed that patriotism was maintained thanks to a 'racial spirit'.

Santos Juliá concludes that it would be quite justifiable to describe the whole process of Nationalist terror as 'genocide' [64]. Comparisons can be made with the even greater genocide launched by the Nazis against their perceived enemies, despite the differences between one regime and the other. Nationalist terror did not compare quantitatively with the Nazi equivalent, but in the ideological justification and intent there were clear similarities. What has distracted from such a comparison has been the peculiar nature of an emerging regime which differed in various ways from its German and Italian counterparts.

The Making of a Leader

Modern biographies of the Nationalist leader, Franco, generally stress the circumstantial nature of his coming to power and his contradictory personality. Few would now challenge the idea that the rebels' would-be head of state rather than being a brilliant military or political leader was, at best, an inveterate opportunist.

The configuration of the new state in the Nationalist zone emerged from the circumstances of the war itself rather than from any pre-war rightist design. The plotters had little time or interest to specify in advance what kind of regime they intended to install, other than their general commitment to 're-establish' order, crush democratic institutions and uphold patriotic and national ideals.

While the rebels and their sympathisers all favoured the establishment of an authoritarian regime, opinions differed as to whether
this would be a republic, a monarchy or a corporate fascist state
[177, 198].

The first step towards a new state structure was the naming of a
military Junta of National Defence. Reflecting the ideological
ambiguity of the rebels, the Junta declared itself non-party; its
vague programme effectively advocated a government similar to
Primo de Rivera's and declared that its principal aim was to rid
Spain of 'soviets' [194]. The Junta's first decree, the Law of
Military Rebellion, determined that those who opposed the uprising were rebelling against the established order, given the supposed
illegitimacy of the Popular Front government. This law would
remain in force until 1969. Other measures included the banning
of all left-wing organisations and the rescinding of the Republic's
reforming legislation. At a local level, all Popular Front authorities
were dismissed, if not detained and shot. They were usually
replaced by Administrative Committees made up of rightists,
usually Falangists but also members of the CEDA or the Radical
Party [176].

What would really give the emergent state an identity and coher-
ence was the appointment of Franco as head of both the army and
the state. It was clear to the military leaders that unity had to be
maintained in order to achieve victory. Also the Germans and
Italians were pressurising for there to be one leader. With Calvo
Sotelo and Generals Sanjurjo and Manuel Goded dead, Jose
Antonio Primo de Rivera in prison and Gil Robles discredited, there
were few candidates to be the supreme chief the Nationalists sought.
Many generals were monarchists, so neither Mola nor Gonzalo
Quiepo de Llano, who respectively controlled the northern and
southern zones, could be trusted owing to their republicanism.
Franco himself also sympathised with the monarchists but he had no
intention of handing power over to them. Instead he would be pragmatic enough to play one faction of the rebels' supporters off
against another in order to ensure his control. Franco's acceptance
of the Monarchist flag as the flag of the rebellion, for instance,
helped sustain Alfonsine hopes of restoration [177].

Despite Franco being driven by 'almost unlimited ambition'
[185], this was not so transparent at first. True to his cautious style,
he had been reluctant to join the plotters and did not commit

109

himself until a few days before the uprising. Franco did not become leader because of his political programme or initiatives. He gave the impression that he was in no hurry to take on so much responsibility. But it was his cold calculating personality, rather than any modesty, that led him to display this apparent indifference. He accordingly bided his time and made sure he remained at the head of his African troops [185, 198].

Franco had a complex and inscrutable character. While he forged an intense relationship with his mother at an early age, it is suggested that his rejection of his father as a drunkard and a wastrel explained his puritanical, cold and vengeful personality [172]. Franco's cruelty was most clearly seen in his lack of any concern for the appalling slaughter being carried out in the rearguard. Despite the claims of his hagiographers, he never agonised over the daily chore of signing death certificates. It was Franco, rather than his brother-in-law Ramón Serrano Suñer, as many believed, who performed this task in person. As it was, he had plenty of collaborators who were prepared to carry out the repression which he sanctioned, and was able, publicly at least, to distance himself, like Hitler, from the actual process.

Franco's psychological profile may explain some of his peculiar traits and authoritarian tendencies, but it does not explain him becoming leader. For a nascent regime that ultimately depended on the army, he was an obvious choice. As the youngest general in the history of the Spanish army, he had distinguished himself as Commander of the Army of Africa, which he now led in the 're-conquest' of the fatherland. Franco had also won respect for his suppression of the Asturias uprising in 1934 [74]. Although his grasp of strategy has been greatly exaggerated, as a military leader he had 'remarkable power to lift those around him' [185]. In what proved to be a master-stroke on the road to becoming *Caudillo* (supreme chief), Franco moved quickly to establish himself as the main interlocutor for both Italians and Germans and was soon recognised by their governments as the leader of the uprising [131, 132].

From August 1936 onwards, Franco became the object of increasing, at first spontaneous, exaltation as supreme military leader. His victories in the push towards Madrid, and in the Church having denominated the war as a 'Crusade', of which he would be portrayed as the heroic leader, encouraged this adulation. A defining moment would be his decision to divert his army in order to relieve the Alcázar in Toledo (see p. 38), making him an internationally known figure virtually overnight.

On 21 September 1936 the Junta of National Defence named Franco as supreme military commander (*Generalísimo*) and head of the government of the Spanish state (*Caudillo*). His position as *Caudillo* was clearly meant to ape the role of the *Duce* or *Führer*, to whom he compared himself. The arguments given by the rebels for the naming of one supreme leader were basically military. At this stage it was not clear what would happen after the war and Franco was still considered by many of his comrades as 'first among equals'. In fact, at the time of his naming as supreme head of the rebel forces no one thought that it would be permanent, except perhaps Franco himself. He had personally crossed out the words 'while the war lasts' in the decree which nominated him head of state. His attainment of near total power has been described as a 'coup within the coup', but this ignores the fact that, by October if not before, the real centre of power was around his person, despite the creation of the Junta of National Defence [185, 198].

Franco's first decree was to name a Technical Junta, an early version of the balancing act that would characterise his regime for the next twenty years, and demonstrated that he could chose ministers for other reasons than competence. The fact that Alfonsine monarchists and generals who were very loyal to Franco formed the core of this proto-government gave an indication of how he saw the new state evolving.

Not surprisingly, Franco's lack of ideological foundation or perspective was still evident despite his newly acquired power. His speeches consisted of basic military-style harangues with vague references to the need for a 'unity of ideas'. The *Caudillo's* limited intellectual horizons reflected, in part, the person who had most influence over his ideological and moral formation, José Millán Astray, the demented founder of the Foreign Legion [38]. However, by the end of 1936 various factors combined to define the emerging profile of the new regime. The transformation of the war into a long, drawn-out struggle forced the rebels to clarify what they were fighting for, as well as against. The Nationalists' increasingly important German and Italian backers also pressurised for a more defined leadership and state structure. An entire propaganda apparatus was thus erected devoted to the inflation of the myth of

111

Franco. He was now portrayed as the all-seeing military genius and great Catholic crusader who would save Spain and Europe from communism. Franco may have seen himself as a warrior-king from Spain's medieval past, a warrior of God against the infidel, but a more earthly form of political organisation would be needed to consolidate his power.

Political Unification

The political unity enforced by Nationalists contrasted with the chronic divisions afflicting their enemies. The creation of a unified party strengthened Franco's hold over the emerging state. But it was destined to play a secondary role rather than being the lynch-pin of the state like its Italian and German counterparts, to which it bore only a superficial resemblance.

The outbreak of war and the emergence of an authoritarian military regime conditioned the immediate future of the Spanish Right. Even prior to the rebellion, the CEDA was in the process of disintegration. Despite forming its own militia, this grouped together barely 6,000 men, played little part in events and was even persecuted by its Falangist rivals. In February 1937, Gil Robles, who spent the war in exile in Portugal, formally dissolved his party. Most other conservative groups and leaders also tended to support the uprising. On the conspiratorial right, the Alfonsine monarchists' presence in ruling-class circles, especially amongst officers close to Franco, meant they would continue to be influential. The Carlists, given their mass base and their militia, were more important at a military level than their Alfonsine rivals. Carlist plans to launch their own uprising had finally been abandoned in favour of collaborating with Mola in their northern stronghold of Navarre. However, they strove to maintain their political independence. The Carlists tried to lay the basis for a corporatist state, launching the *Obra Corporatista Nacional* (National Corporative Effort) and their own military academy. They also took unilateral decisions, such as legalising the Jesuits, published their own War Bulletin and issued decrees. In their press the Carlists initially described the pretender Javier de Borbón-Parma, rather than Franco, as the *Caudillo* [5].

Had the uprising triumphed at once, the traditional Right would probably have been more important in the new regime. But the war proved the catalyst that was to convert the relatively marginal Falange into a mass party [184, 197]. As a more national, homogeneous and popular force, the Falange rapidly became the most important political organisation in the Nationalist zone. It provided thousands of militia and played a central role in purging the rearguard. In many areas it was created by the coup and was financed by local oligarchies. The upsurge of support for the Falange was also due to its dynamic and efficient propaganda. Following the example of fascist movements elsewhere, as Sheelagh Ellwood explains, the Falange's 'daring modernist aesthetic', with its many formats, effectively conveyed fascist ideas and images to the population [178]. The Falange could also attract secular support from anti-liberal and anti-Communist elements that did not look towards traditional clerical Spain. The promises of 'social revolution' combined with the need to escape repression even favoured the incorporation of leftists trapped in the Nationalist zone [194].

With a central military authority under Franco established and all potential opposition eliminated or imprisoned, the new regime still needed to consolidate its base through the creation of some form of political force. Franco's brother and his then main advisor, Nicolás, had already advocated the formation of a 'Francoist' party in August 1936. But Franco had rejected the idea, as he feared it would end up like the corrupt and ineffective party of the Primo dictatorship, *Unión Patriotica*. The arrival of the talented Serrano Suñer in the Nationalist zone in February 1937 accelerated the process towards political unification. Serrano, a former CEDA member now sympathetic to the Nazis, soon became Franco's closest advisor, and architect of the new party [197]. Many right-wing leaders were persuaded of the pressing need for political unification by the defeat at Guadalajara, which showed there would be no quick victory.

Even the Carlists had ceased to be an obstacle to unity once Franco stamped on their attempts to form their own Military Academy. With the more pliant Count Rodezno as leader, Carlist insistence on a monarchist solution had abated. The situation in the Falange was more complicated. With the party's unprecedented growth, its leadership had adopted an arrogant attitude towards the other right-wing organisations. It favoured the dissolution of the rest of the Right rather than unification as such. However, the Falange's ideological stance was increasingly contradictory. While

113

insisting on the revolutionary character of the party, its sympathy with other totalitarian parties and its aspiration for total power, the Falange also identified with the Catholic 'crusade' that was underway. The differences with other rightist forces tended to blur as the war progressed. Moreover, once the Falange realised it could not do without Franco and the army and had to take the Carlists into account, unification was unavoidable.

The fusion of the different forces into one party was made easier by the absence of the Falange's leader Jose Antonio Primo de Rivera. He had been jailed before the war, in March 1936, and was executed in November. Contrary to subsequent myth, Franco had never had any sort of close relationship with Jose Antonio, who regarded him as 'pompous, self-obsessed and possessed of a caution verging on cowardice' [185]. With its leader in Nationalist territory Franco would have never dominated the Falange, thus he did little to save him from execution. When Jose Antonio's death was finally made public two years later, the ground had been laid for the idea that Franco was the true heir of Spanish fascism.

In the absence of José Antonio, leadership had passed to Manuel Hedilla, who, along with other old-guard Falangists, opposed the dilution of the fascist party into a unified body. It is suggested that Hedilla and his supporters were probably encouraged by the German *chargé d'affairs*, General Wihelm Faupel, to oppose any compromise with Catholic conservatism [82]. Hedilla had little experience and, moreover, his authority was undermined from within the Falange, principally by the self-styled 'legitimist' section headed by José Antonio's sister, Pilar Primo de Rivera [38]. Franco, in turn, was irritated by the revolutionary tone of much Falangist propaganda, which favoured a national-syndicalist state. Worse still, Hedilla insisted on hailing José Antonio as *Caudillo*.

Neither the Falange nor the Carlists were warned or consulted concerning Franco's plans, and in the second week of April 1937 he simply announced his decision to unify all rightist parties. The Falange, distracted by its own internal disputes and with a blind faith in its strength and importance, was unable to react. Although the new party, the *Falange Española Tradicionalista de las JONS* (FET), kept most of the Falange's programme, of the old guard only Hedilla was in its leadership. The other five Falangists included, along with the four Carlists, were all close to Franco's General Headquarters. If Hedilla had accepted participation he would have been seen as handing over the Falange to Franco. Both his own supporters and the 'legitimists' pressured him not to take up his post. After a few violent incidents involving party loyalists, Hedilla was arrested, expelled from the organisation and imprisoned, accused of organising a coup. Although Falangists predominated in the new party and it was usually simply referred to as the 'Falange', ideologically its programme was an amalgam of fascist corporatism and – reflecting Franco's own preferences – *Acción Española*'s Catholic traditionalism [22, 178, 184, 197].

References in the founding programme to the need for an authoritarian state appeared to follow Falangist thinking, but the deliberate avoidance of the term 'party' in favour of a 'new political entity' did not. More of a movement than a homogeneous party, the FET was designed to play a supporting role to Franco's dictatorship. The unified party's appointed leadership, the National Council, had little power. Half the former Falangists appointed to serve on it were recent recruits and thinly disguised monarchists [185]. Declaring that he was only accountable 'before God and history', Franco treated the National Council as 'advisory'. The complete identity of the FET with Franco was such that the date of its foundation became celebrated as the 'Day of the *Caudillo*'.

The FET's principal task during and immediately after the war was the control and 'cleansing' of, first, the rearguard and then the whole of the country. In Franco's first government the Falange held the ministries of Agriculture and Labour. Given the centrality of Agrarian Reform and industrial unrest in the origins of the war, control of these two ministries fitted with the Falange's leading role in repressing the enemies of the new Spain. From the Ministry of Agriculture it oversaw the dismantling of the Republic's Agrarian Reform. From the Labour Ministry it laid the basis for the future system of 'vertical' trade unions (see p. 125).

An important subsidiary organisation of the FET was the *Sección Femenina* (SF), the only non-Catholic women's organisation permitted in the Nationalist zone. Although Jose Antonio Primo de Rivera had little to say about the role of women, the SF, from being a marginal subsection of the Falange, grew to become a massive organisation during the war with nearly 600,000 members [191]. Its structure was modelled on the Nazi women's organisation the *Reichsfrauenführung* and some of its leaders maintained close relations with the Germans, even after unification [82]. But as a mass organisation, the SF's membership was imbued with the very strong religious spirit prevalent in the Nationalist zone [182].

As on the opposing side, women were mobilised on a grand scale, principally by the SF, to work in medical, food and other relief services. By late 1938, the SF dispensed 10 million meals per month to adults and children. Its responsibilities soon included the organisation of *Auxiliar Social* (Social Aid), initially created by Falangist Mercedes Sanz-Bachiller [39]. Effectively a female equivalent of military service, it became obligatory for all women between the ages of 17 and 35. Women who did not complete this service were debarred from state or local government jobs. For the emerging regime *Auxiliar Social* proved a useful tool through which to exercise social control.

Although the Falange competed with the Church in the field of imposing female role models, the party's women's section was also an important tool for the indoctrination of women in a more general sense. There was an obvious contradiction between the SF's insistence that women's role was in the home as devoted mothers and the reality that its leading members were 'public' figures [179, 182, 191]. The same contradiction was evident in the mass mobilisation of, albeit unmarried, women for public service, or its encouragement to women to enter higher education. According to Inbal Ofer, the SF, by using its relative organisational autonomy, offered an image of femininity that took into account its members' self-perceptions not only as women but also, by appropriating 'virile attributes' such as 'heroism, forcefulness and intelligence', as Falangists. The war gave women the 'chance to die for the fatherland' and martyrs were usually referred to as 'virile'. There were even a few cases of SF members joining combat groups [183].

Yet the SF's independence was very limited and it never in any fundamental sense challenged gender roles as determined by the Church, state and party. There was no female equivalent of the 'new fascist man' proclaimed by Falangist ideologues [199]. Its leader, Pilar Primo de Rivera, never advocated anything that could disturb the deeply reactionary and patriarchal views of the doyens of the new state [38].

The creation of this hybrid unified party was a great victory for Franco. He had managed to get his embryonic state to take over all existing political organisations and had shown unexpected political qualities to back up his 'greed for power' [198]. Franco's sense of timing, and duplicity in carrying out the forced unification, proved essential to the consolidation of his political authority. The other key ingredient of the consolidation of his regime would be the blessing of the Church.

A Religious Crusade

The Catholic Church was essential to the rebels' winning legitimacy and truly mass support. Despite 'defence of the fatherland', not religion, being the initial reason given to justify the rebellion, it soon became obvious that, other than to defend their faith, Catholicism was the 'ideal focus' for anyone who wanted to protect their own interests and social position [29]. With the partial exception of the Falange, all the political forces that supported the rebellion were fiercely Catholic in their beliefs. When it came to winning popular backing beyond the elites that endorsed the uprising, religion was the key factor and was soon skilfully exploited by the rebels. Once Franco became aware of the importance of the Church for his consolidation as head of state his public religiosity increased accordingly. He would turn to the Church, rather than the Falange, to define the social content of his regime. Hence the Church, especially after the war, would become the central ideological prop of the regime, giving it legitimacy and a ready-made set of all-encompassing ideas and theories. It also provided the totalitarian infrastructure that the FET alone was not able to provide; penetrating every area of daily life and exercising a control over people that would be the envy of any authoritarian one-party state. For the populace, demonstrating religious piety and belief became another way to survive, to get a job and some minimal level of security, however bad the conditions.

The Church itself has always justified its support for the Nationalists as a reaction to the anti-clerical legislation of the Republic and the persecution it suffered both before and during the war. In the influential Collective Letter, signed by the majority of bishops on 1 July 1937, the war was presented as a confrontation between good and evil. The Church was an 'innocent, peaceful, defenceless victim' of war and, faced with being totally destroyed by communism, had no choice but to back the uprising. The Collective Letter had an extraordinary effect on the Catholic world in rallying support for Franco as the 'guardian of Christian civilisation'. The Church's wartime martyrdom would be a constant feature of its discourse in years to come.

The liberal Catholic historian Hilari Raguer points to 'savage religious persecution' at the beginning of the war as the main reason why the Church supported the rebels, despite its 'great responsibility' for the growing radicalisation before the war [187]. However, the Church had already fully committed itself to the rising before clear news of the anti-clerical onslaught in the Republican zone reached rebel-held territory [174]. A more decisive reason for this support was that, with few exceptions, the Church hierarchy was not just opposed to the Republic as such but was indifferent to representative democracy as a whole. Like most of the rebels' supporters, the Church wanted to return to the situation prior to 1931 [7]. The clergy were not somehow innocent bystanders, as the Church would always claim. Any caution shown by the Church in the first weeks of the war had more to do with apprehension about the influence of the Falange than any doubts about the coup. Clerical enthusiasm for the uprising was reflected in the increasingly elaborate liturgical events organised to ask for God's blessing of the rebel cause [171, 190]. As Julian Casanova concludes, the Church was 'delighted that arms were used to ensure "material order", liquidate the unfaithful and return its freedom' [174].

Most importantly, the transformation of the war into a 'crusade' to save Christian civilisation provided a binding, unitary sense of purpose for the disparate elements that backed the uprising [177]. It also served to cover up the class origins of the war [71, 188]. The term 'crusade', long used by the Carlists in their struggle against liberal Spain, began to be used as early as August 1936 by members of the Church hierarchy. By dying in defence of the faith, for a crusade, the Nationalist troops became martyrs. As Mary Vincent explains, this martyrdom provided a powerful agglutinate by bringing together a 'specifically Spanish vision of masculinity and Catholic notions of abnegation and transcendental reward, with a sense of sacrifice that was both heroic and patriotic' [199].

For Franco, winning support from the Vatican was of immense long-term political importance. At the outset, the Vatican did not want to take sides and Pope Pio XI's first pronouncement on the war attacked its inhumanity, in general, and proposed 'peace and forgiveness' [7, 101]. The Vatican still had misgivings about the Nationalist cause, particularly the growing Nazi influence over the rebels and the treatment of Basque clergy. Inside Spain, the Church hierarchy had been quick to condemn the Basque priests' support for the loyalists. Two dozen would be shot by the rebels, with sanctions imposed on 700 during the course of the war for 'collaborating with Communism' [70]. But these doubts would not last. When the Vatican took up Azaña's proposal in spring 1937 for a negotiated peace, the Spanish cardinal Isidro Gomà persuaded the Holy See not to take part. The threat of Communism and, in particular, anti-clerical violence, convinced the Vatican to recognise the Nationalist government in August 1937. The Vatican remained uneasy about aspects of Franco's regime, such as the subordination of Catholic associations to the Spanish state and the dictator's desire to re-establish regal power, meaning his own, over Church appointees. The death of Pio XI in early 1939 led to a closer relationship between the Nationalist government and the Vatican. The new Pope, Pius XII, warmly welcomed Franco's victory [101].

According to William Callahan, the repression being carried out in the Nationalist rearguard raised a moral dilemma for the clergy [7]. However, only a few, most notably Bishop Olaechea, called for mercy and those that did were deported or punished. In fact, despite claims to the contrary, the Church was fully aware of the extent and nature of Nationalist terror [174]. The majority of the clergy not only approved but also collaborated in the repression, usually by denouncing individuals to the authorities or refusing to vouch for the good conduct of suspects [64]. In a few cases, priests even participated directly in the killing [174]. The Church also played its part in covering up for the slaughter. As we have seen, many deaths were not inscribed in any official register; instead the Church offered families the opportunity to record them as long as the victims were inscribed as 'natural' deaths [180]. Above all, under the blanket justification of a Holy War, religious piety meant those carrying out murder could have a clean conscience [196]. Finally, priests were active in pressurising condemned prisoners, using all forms of emotional blackmail, to repent before execution. The Church was delighted to report that up to 90 per cent of prisoners agreed to do so [188]. Once the war was over, the Church made no gesture in favour of forgiveness or reconciliation. More the opposite; most clergy were deeply involved in denouncing suspects and keeping the crusade going. The Church also white-washed life in the regime's prisons and camps for external consumption. Catholic propaganda spoke of how there was no torture, no murder, and those who ran the prison system were decent citizens [174].

Supporters of *Acción Española* developed a specifically Catholic ideological outlook to sustain the new state. 'National Catholicism' combined a consistently conservative interpretation of Church doctrine with the anti-Communist and Spanish centralist principles of the crusade, in which the state and Church fused into 'one entity'. There was a common exaltation of Catholic, fascist and military values of order, *Caudillaje* and religion. According to its architects, National Catholicism had deep and distant roots in the history of Spain. The decadence of Spanish society had been caused by foreign heresies such as Protestantism, Liberalism and Socialism [194]. Later, with the relative decline in the importance of the Falange, parallel to the defeat of the Axis powers in the Second World War, National Catholicism became the central ideological underpinning of Franco's dictatorship.

The Church had 'two great obsessions' during the war: Christianisation and education [7]. The latter was handed over in its entirety to the ecclesiastical authorities. This was one of the clearest examples of the difference from fascist Italy or Nazi Germany, where the party dominated education. In October 1936, a Commission on Culture and Teaching was established in the Nationalist zone with the aim of re-Christianising schools and eliminating Republican teachers. The previous state education system was closed down and 75 per cent of teachers were accused of betraying the nation. There was a systematic purge and over 50,000 schoolteachers were eventually sacked [7, 176], thus leading to a serious lack of staff. As a result, schools would be overwhelmingly staffed by religious personnel, in particular nuns. Education was now firmly based on Catholic teaching with the added ingredient of the formation of a 'national spirit' in the hands of the Falange. Through education, the Church aimed at ensuring resignation and respect for order and social hierarchy.

The Church also rapidly established its ideological control over questions of morality, the family and gender. Notions of gender were used both explicitly and implicitly in the construction of the Francoist crusade. In the Nationalist zone, women were portrayed as intellectually and physically inferior to men. Righteous women were essentially either virgins or good mothers. The thoroughly patriarchal construct of Nationalist thinking inevitably contrasted dominant masculine role models to female ones. Clerically inspired propaganda insisted that 'cleansing Spain' would be a 'manly' task and spoke of (male) Spaniards' 'legendary virility'. According to Mary Vincent, 'disturbances in both gender roles and the prevailing moral order' threatened not only the family and society in general but even the state itself [199]. Women were expected to be modest and austere. The purity of women contrasted with the view that the body was a source of dirtiness, contamination and corruption of men. However, extramarital and illicit sexual activities flourished in the backstreets and bars frequented by soldiers. Prostitution was a serious problem, the proliferation of which the authorities were generally helpless to curb.

Repression specifically aimed at women would never have been possible without the agreement and justification provided by the Catholic establishment [180]. According to the Church, the Republican side wanted 'neither God nor masters' and its female supporters rejected both parents and husbands; they were unfeminine and, above all, un-Spanish' [174, 199]. The ideologue of National Catholicism, José Maria Pemán, described 'red' women as full of brutality and criminal instincts and as more sexually active than what was considered 'normal'. This 'devaluation of the spirit led to prostitution, free love and a decline of childbirth caused by the dissolute germs of a deeply rooted evil' [188]; all of which could only be cured by religion, and regeneration of the family. The social policies of Nationalist Spain made sure these categories became 'reality'. Many women, destitute without their dead or imprisoned husbands or fathers, had little choice but to prostitute themselves. In this way, right-wing prejudices about 'red' women's morality were confirmed while, at the same time, a useful 'service' was provided for a male-dominated society riddled with hypocrisy.

The family, along with the municipality and the syndicate, was held up by National Catholicism as one of the 'natural units' of the society now being established in the 'true Spain'. To protect the family, the Nationalists repealed the Republic's divorce law. Many couples who had separated now found that they were 'married' again with all that that implied, especially for women, who were to be totally subordinated legally to their husbands. Women were also

121

'liberated from the workshop', in part because economic circumstances were more favourable in the Nationalist zone than in the opposing one and female labour was not so essential, but also because of the insistence that mothers should be fulfilling their traditional role as homemakers. Catholic-inspired legislation deemed that women's education would be separate and subordinated to preparing them for their domestic role [182]. Girls could only be taught by women teachers, which given the lack of women with a university education, meant that they would get a less academic education than boys.

Victory for Franco hence brought with it the most important privileges that the Spanish Church had enjoyed in the modern age. The Catholic hierarchy would reciprocate by providing the backbone of his regime.

The New Spain

By the end of the war, many of the administrative and ideological pillars of Franco's regime were in place. Despite the corporatist paraphernalia, the core ideas behind the new state's social and economic policies were a continuation of the aims of the traditional Right and the oligarchy. The regime's adherence to fascism was tempered by the eventual defeat of the Axis powers, and the centrality of National Catholicism would become even clearer. Fascist or not, the emergent regime was based on the most savage exploitation of the working class. This took place in the context of the institutionalisation of the 'two Spains'. The punishment and ostracism of the defeated would be perpetuated long after the war's end. Millions of ordinary Spaniards, in a context of massive material deprivation after three years of war, would suffer the consequences of the dictatorship's punitive social, economic and political policies for decades to come.

Programmatically, the emergent Nationalist state did not represent a break with the politics of the mainstream Right in the pre-war years. The official ideology of the new regime reflected the heterogeneous nature of the coalition that provided its power base. Nationalist ideology was an instrument to bind together the disparate elements that supported it. Newer fascist concepts of race were thus combined with more traditional Spanish conservative ideas. Anti-Communism and defence of 'Christian civilisation' were central themes of Nationalist propaganda, as was the concept of a 'spiritual, social and historic fatherland' locked in mortal combat with its antithesis. It was a unified and culturally homogeneous fatherland in which national values were incarnated in the romanticised figure of the *labrador* (farmer). Although race, in particular anti-Semitism, was not as central as it was for the Nazis, it was a constant factor of Nationalist propaganda during the war. Nationalist Anti-Semitism has usually been presented as a reflection of German influence over sectors of Spanish fascism or at least an attempt to ingratiate themselves with their German providers. However, it had as much to do with the resuscitation of sixteenth-century Spanish anti-Semitism as with Nazism [39, 183]. Perhaps the most curious element of this hybrid ideology, but something in common with Italian and German right-wing thought, was its stylised mystification of the past. Thus public demonstrations, such as its homages to the *Caudillo* or victory celebrations, were a peculiar mixture of fascist iconography, Catholic ritual and pseudo-medieval pageantry.

The rebels justified their uprising in order to pre-empt a Moscow-inspired Communist revolution, and fake documents purporting to show such a plot's existence were soon in circulation. The myth of a Communist plot served as a unifying factor both internally and especially abroad, where the Nationalists' sympathisers would insist on this justification for the military uprising [68, 196]. By extension, the Republic was sustained by Moscow, whose 'hordes' were flooding across the border, aided by the 'communist' Popular Front government of France. The International Brigades, whose numbers were wildly exaggerated in the rebel press, were said to be guilty of the most horrendous crimes against the Spanish people. In contrast, the presence of far more foreign troops on the Nationalist side was consistently denied or ignored. The strict control over foreign reporters helped keep this fact from being too widely disseminated [100]. Central to the spurious legality of the rebels was the supposedly fraudulent nature of the Popular Front's election victory of February 1936. The subsequent freeing of political prisoners and election of Azaña as President was hence also illegal. As a consequence the uprising was not a rebellion but the re-establishment of legality.

The perception of the war as one against 'foreign invaders'

rather than a civil conflict between Spaniards was, of course, something the Nationalists increasingly had in common with their Popular Front enemies [69]. The very term *nacionales*, used by the rebels to describe themselves, was meant to reinforce the idea that they alone were the true Spaniards. But, despite its dependence on foreign aid, there is no doubt that the Nationalist cause enjoyed widespread and popular support inside Spain itself. Mass support was based not just on the upper echelons of society with most to lose from a reforming Republic, let alone a social revolution, but on those sectors of the middle classes which felt threatened, as they had in Germany and Italy, by a militant and powerful labour movement. Of equal importance was religious faith faced with rampant anti-clericalism. For the deeply conservative peasantry of Castile and northern Spain, defence of both religion and private property bound them inextricably to the rebel cause.

The different Nationalist social constituencies, or at least their elites, were represented in Franco's first government, finally named on 30 January 1938. The army, the dominant partner, had control of military and public order, the Church held education, justice was in the hands of a former Carlist, and a Social Ministry was set up under a Falangist.

Along with the establishment of political and administrative structures, the articulation of an economic policy tailored to serve the emergent regime was a priority. Nationalist policy, as in other areas, reflected the different interests behind the rebellion. Fascist-style corporatism was only one element and was defended by businessmen, the army and Catholic ideologues alike. State encroachment in the economy may have appeared as an offence against entrepreneurship, but it did not mean the regime was not committed to capitalism. The state was to intervene only where needed: in private industries not capable of reaching 'national' objectives.

Fascist anti-capitalist rhetoric hardly survived political unification, and where it did it posed no threat to the priorities of industrialists and businessmen. Most leading Falangists, in fact, adapted without too many problems to rampant capitalism. There was still a rhetorical commitment to social reform but this had more to do with placating the rebels' Nazi and Italian fascist sponsors than any serious intent [185]. In fact, behind the propaganda can be seen the more pragmatic concerns of the ruling classes to preserve private property and their own power to exploit it, without any interference from democratic institutions or workers' organisations.

The limited information available on the economic evolution of the Nationalist zone points to Italian and German aid being central, especially in the absence of any gold reserve [103]. The rebels did not have problems regarding trade, given that there was no effective blockade of rebel-held ports. Trade was not just with the fascist powers, but also with, especially US-based, multinationals. Franco, of course, could assure foreign firms and investors that under a Nationalist government they would be safe from revolutionary upheaval or any sort of threat to their interests. The Nationalists found various ways of serving the huge debts they incurred, mainly through the concession of mining rights and the exporting of raw materials (see pp. 64–5).

The socio-economic basis of the new regime was encapsulated in the *Fuero de Trabajo* (Labour Charter), a 'pseudo constitution' established in March 1938. Although generally assumed to have been inspired by the Italian *Carta del Lavoro*, it was, in fact, more a synthesis of Falangist, Carlist and Portuguese concepts [194]. The original draft was drawn up by the FET but conservative ministers were appalled by its fascistic tone, and two clauses – those relating to the nationalisation of banks and Agrarian Reform – were removed. Once more the programme of the traditional Right prevailed. The *Fuero* did, however, 'abolish the class struggle'. Thus the establishment of all-encompassing labour organisations, the vertical syndicates, would supposedly mean, as in other authoritarian rightist regimes, workers and employers alike putting national above class interests.

At the centre of Franco's economic policy was the concept of self-sufficiency, autarky. It has been assumed that the adoption of autarky was a consequence of Nationalist Spain's isolation but Michael Richards argues that its roots were far more ideological. According to Nationalist propagandists, political, cultural and spiritual regeneration would come through self-imposed isolation from a degenerate world. The purging of Spanish society from top to bottom of the 'anti-Spain' thus meant an economic policy designed to strengthen national survival and eliminate unwanted foreign interference [188].

The relative economic stability in the Nationalist zone allowed the rebel leaders to dedicate their full attention to winning the war.

Measures such as price controls and the production of certain products under government patronage helped stabilise the internal economic infrastructure. Neither did civilians suffer in such a direct way effects of war such as either direct bombardment or continuous blockades. Hence, in general terms, many civilians in the Nationalist zone experienced a relatively secure and stable existence during the war compared with those in the opposing zone. For a minority there was also the advantage of soaring profits and widespread tax fraud. Franco could boast in 1942 how the 'rich had become richer' because the war had saved Spain and thus saved its wealth [178, 188].

The weight of social and economic deprivation fell on the working class and rural poor. Workers were subjected to the most draconian conditions: extremely low pay, long hours and fierce discipline. The aim was that only those who accepted blind obedience survived. However, there were still acts of resistance, such as low-level sabotage and other forms of obstruction. There were even occasional strikes but these were met in the immediate post-war years with severe repression, usually the summary execution of those involved. With production increased substantially in many sectors and salaries severely reduced, the rate of exploitation increased massively. In a situation where prices had doubled between 1936 and 1940 it was impossible to live on the average salary. With the added misery caused by the arbitrary confiscation of their property, many Republican sympathisers became completely destitute [180]. Poverty and lack of sanitation were such that both typhus and tuberculosis were widespread. The Red Cross painted a tremendous picture of hunger and need; children were 'dying like flies' [188]. In all, during the first years of the Franco regime it is estimated that 200,000 people died of hunger.

The regeneration of Spain through the blood sacrifice of its enemies would continue with a vengeance for years to come. There would be no forgiveness and no forgetting. The regime considered itself permanently at war. Emboldened by his triumph, Franco was committed to a 'post-war policy of institutionalised revenge'. In comparison with the other authoritarian regimes of the time that emerged from civil wars, Finland in 1918 and Greece in 1949, Franco's dictatorship would be the only one under which there was such a long 'uncivil' peace [54, 59, 75].

The institutionalisation of repression and protection of existing elites was rapidly formalised through the passing of a series of totalitarian measures. As, according to the Nationalists, this was not a war but a struggle between 'the spirit of Spain and a materialist deviation of its history' there was no juridical or moral equality between the two sides [180, 193]. A clear example of this was the Law of Responsibilities passed in February 1939, aimed at those guilty of the crime of supporting the 'illegitimate' Republic. The law was retroactive to October 1934 but in practice even those involved in agitation in 1909 or 1917 were persecuted. This legislation aimed at punishing not just active supporters of the Republican cause, but all those guilty of 'grave passivity', a useful catch-all to drag into the repressive net even more of those suspected of not being loyal enough to the new Spain. The lack of legal guarantees, typical of authoritarian states, created a generalised sense of fear and left the field open for corruption [188].

At the end of the war it is calculated there were 270,000 prisoners in Spain's jails and concentration camps [175, 192]. Conditions were appalling. Although the level of genocidal murder did not compare quantitatively with their Nazi counterparts, the Nationalists adopted a similar philosophy in relation to the inmates. Over-work, an appalling diet and lack of the most basic sanitation and medical care guaranteed a high death rate [188]. Overcrowded prisons, combined with the declining fortunes of the Axis powers, probably contributed to the gradual decline in executions [193]. As in Germany, the jail and camp system was connected to economic activities and thousands of prisoners worked as slave labour. Women detainees continued to be abused. Particularly traumatic was the regime's policy of taking children from their imprisoned mothers and sending them to Catholic-run orphanages or having them adopted to make sure they had a decent patriotic upbringing [200].

The consequence of this multi-faceted and all-pervasive policy of repression was not only the physical, but the psychological crushing of the Republican population as Franco had intended. The regime provoked an obsession with mere survival. People found refuge in forgetting. So the defeat was more than just a military one. For the vanquished there was the loss of their past, their identity, ideals, dignity and vision of the future. Terror demanded the breaking of links of friendship and social solidarity. The only way individuals could cross the barrier between winners and losers and show they were not part of the anti-Spain was by denouncing someone else [175, 176, 195].

The regime that emerged in the Nationalist zone during the war does not fit easily into any predefined schema [75, 133, 175, 184, 194]. Despite having the external trappings of its fascist and Nazi benefactors, what has become identified as 'Francoism' was essentially a coalition of different and, at times, conflicting interests. This coalition of interests – industrialists, landowners, the Church, the army, Falange and monarchists – excluded by definition those that had not been on the winning side. The various tendencies, usually referred to as the 'families' of the regime, were represented in the 'plurality' of ministers. When the war ended, despite his unlimited power, Franco still had to take into account the relatively autonomous sectors on which he based his strength. Franco was, on the one hand, the non-fascist head of a fascist party that supposedly aspired 'to make reality its revolutionary rhetoric' and, on the other, the commander of an army whose most eminent figures considered him 'first among equals'. He did not achieve complete and final control of both the party and the army until the early 1940s [194].

According to Richards, the true nature of Francoism can be found within the framework of the regime's economic policy, the elaboration of its myths and its ideology and the experience of the day-to-day life of the defeated [188]. The rhetoric of fascism was certainly ever-present. Francoism had many of the characteristics of fascism: the elimination of democracy, destruction of the workers' movement, a one-party state, a personality cult around the leader, the mobilisation of mass support, the rhetoric of state paternalism, corporatism and racism. Yet it is clearly the case that Franco adopted the trappings of contemporary fascism to suit his own purposes. There were elements which set his regime apart from the Italian or German model, most obviously the aforementioned coalition of interests represented in Franco's governments, the influence of a profoundly reactionary Church and the central political role of the army.

In reality it was a hybrid authoritarian regime, which aimed, like fascism, to secure complete freedom of action for the ruling oligarchy through the untrammelled exploitation of the working classes. But it was not a static regime and would mutate during the nearly forty years of its existence. It adapted itself to the context in which it found itself, hence the regime's later ability to develop economically, while maintaining its prime role as protector of the traditional elites. An estimated 350,000 Spanish citizens had died in the war, many the victims of repression, out of a total population of around 25 million. Franco took over a devastated and profoundly divided country – a division he would do his utmost to perpetuate. For the majority of the Spanish people the long haul towards democracy and modernisation would drag on painfully for another forty years.

6 Conclusions

The complexities of the Spanish Civil War are such that despite the extensive literature that has been produced over the years, potentially fruitful research can still be carried out. In this sense, work on cultural history and the exploration of memory are important developments, especially when integrated into a more general overview of the conflict and its causes. At the level of military history, the war in the north and the organisation, role and characteristics of the popular militias on both sides merit further investigation. In the international context, the opening of the former Soviet archives has in recent years enriched historians' work on the conflict. Of course, a lot more remains to be done, in particular in relation to the activities of the Soviet and other secret services.

With the partial exception of Barcelona, satisfactory social histories of Madrid and other cities during the war have yet to be produced. The realities of everyday existence in both rearguards is now being considered by historians and can provide an important new dimension to understanding how the war affected the whole of the population and not just its leading actors. Also, the history of the Republic following the crisis of May 1937 is only recently attracting the attention it deserves. Finally, the opening up and reorganisation of archives in Spain itself over the past two decades continue to present new opportunities. In this context the inaccessibility, as yet, of some ecclesiastical archives means, despite important new studies on the Church in 1930s Spain, this remains an area open to further interpretation and analysis.

When drawing conclusions from the different aspects of the history of the Civil War, certain elements stand out. During the pre-war years the evident refusal of the oligarchy and the Right, and not only its 'conspiratorial' factions, to accept even the most minimal social and political reform made modernising and democratising the country extremely problematic. The corresponding radicalisation of organised labour, compounded by the spread of fascism throughout Europe, further reduced the margin for a gradual and piecemeal process of change. Although civil war was not inevitable, to avoid it would have meant either the renunciation of the whole reform process or pre-emptive and decisive action by the Left.

Few would challenge the view that military strategy on both sides was determined by broader political agendas. Franco's slow and exterminatory war aimed to regenerate Spain through the physical elimination and psychological crushing of the Republic's social base. For the Republic, the subordination of military strategy to both maintaining internal order and winning over the Western democracies meant the failure to explore alternative military strategies. In particular it meant squandering the revolutionary enthusiasm of the early months of the war. The only time full-scale popular mobilisation was used for military ends, during the siege of Madrid, was an example of how this enthusiasm could have been successfully integrated into the loyalist war effort.

At an international level the decisive contribution of military aid to Franco's victory is underscored by recent research. Likewise it is now clear that the democracies, particularly Britain, were never going to support the Republic, whatever its configuration. This intrinsic hostility of the democracies, or at least of their ruling circles, undermined the whole basis of the loyalists' commitment to obtaining their support at the expense of all other considerations. Similarly, it is hard to escape the conclusion that the Soviet government's fundamental motivation was self-interest, despite the evidently contradictory elements of Soviet policy during the war. While anti-Communist accounts of Soviet intervention have been shown to be too linear, if not simplistic, there is a danger in some newer studies of discounting its effects altogether. The introduction of Stalinist methods and politics into the Spanish conflict compounded the already deep internal divisions that prefigured the outbreak of war.

The polemic over the relationship between the war and the revolution will no doubt continue, albeit enriched by recent histories, but certain elements still stand out. In particular, the weakness, evident in November 1933 and July 1936, of the petty bourgeois political groupings on which the Popular Front strategy relied. Instead, resistance to the rebellion was provided more or less exclusively by an organised working class which was expected, or forced, to sacrifice its long-standing demands for social justice and equality in the name of placating middle-class opinion both at home and abroad. Finally, recent histories deepen our understanding of the emergent Francoist regime. Despite it not fitting neatly into any predefined schema, its profoundly conservative and punitive character is beyond doubt. The pivotal role of the Church in providing the ideological and social infrastructure of the dictatorship is also clearer than ever.

Abandoned to their fate by the democracies, both during and long after the war, many Spanish people would pay dearly for having dared to challenge the entrenched interests of traditional elites. The long night of Francoism, followed by the strictures of the *pacto de olvido* during the transition to democracy (1975–1977), means that only now are the terrible memories of the past being finally disinterred for the descendants of the hundreds of thousands victims of war and dictatorship.

Bibliography

Origins and Background

[1] M. Alpert, 'The Spanish Army and the Popular Front', in M. S. Alexander and H. Graham, *The French and Spanish Popular Fronts: Comparative Perspectives* (Cambridge, 1989). Instructive essay on the differing reasons why the Army turned against the Republic.

[2] J. Arostegui (et al.), *La militarización de la política durante la II República: Teoría y práctica de la violencia en la España de los años treinta, Historia Contemporanea*, no. 11 (Bilbao, 1994). Collection of essays on barely studied pre-war paramilitary organisations.

[3] S. Ben-Ami, *Fascism from Above: The Dictatorship of Primo de Rivera in Spain, 1923–1930* (Oxford, 1983). Still the best account of the Primo de Rivera dictatorship. See also [4].

[4] S. Ben-Ami, 'The Crisis of the Dynastic Élite in the Transition from Monarchy to Republic, 1929–1931', in F. Lannon and P. Preston (eds), *Elites and Power in Twentieth-Century Spain: Essays in Honour of Sir Raymond Carr* (Oxford, 1990).

[5] M. Blinkhorn, *Carlism and Crisis in Spain, 1931–1939* (Cambridge, 1975). Unsurpassed history of Carlism in the 1930s.

[6] C. Borderias, 'Women Workers in the Barcelona Labour Market, 1856–1936', in A. Smith (ed.), *Red Barcelona: Social Protest and Labour Mobilization in the Twentieth Century* (London, 2002). On the transformation of women's lives with their integration into the labour market. See also [41].

[7] W. J. Callahan, *The Catholic Church in Spain, 1875–1998* (Washington, D.C., 2000). Well-researched history from a liberal Catholic viewpoint. See also [29] and [187]. Contrast, in part, with [174].

[8] R. Carr, *Spain, 1808–1975* (Oxford, 1982). Classic history of modern Spain.

[9] S. Christie, *We the Anarchists! A Study of the Iberian Anarchist Federation (FAI), 1927–1937* (Hastings, 2000). Sympathetic account of the FAI's journey from anarchist purism to wartime pragmatism. See also [164]. Contrast with [143].

[10] B. Clavero, P. Ruiz Torres and F. J. Hernández Montalbán, *Estudios sobre la revolución burguesa en España* (Madrid, 1979). Three studies on different aspects of Spain's bourgeois revolution.

Bibliography

[11] C. Cobb, 'The Republican State and Mass Educational–Cultural Initiatives, 1931–1936', in H. Graham and J. Labanyi, *Spanish Cultural Studies: An Introduction* (Oxford, 1995). Useful brief introduction to the Republic's educational reform. See also [24].

[12] G. A. Collier, *Socialists of Rural Andalucia* (Stanford, 1987). Interesting case study of Socialist organisation and land workers' lives and struggles in one Andalusian village.

[13] J. Diez Medrano, *Divided Nation: Class, Politics and Nationalism in the Basque Country and Catalonia* (New York, 1995). The national question past to present. See also [21] and [44].

[14] M. Delgado, 'Violencia anticlerical e iconoclasta en la España contemporánea', in R. Cruz (et al.), *Culturas y políticas de la violencia. España siglo XX* (Madrid, 2005). Anthropological essay which locates the origins of anti-clericalism in gender and cultural identity. See also [34] and [171].

[15] A. Durgan, 'The 1933 Elections in Spain and the Defeat of the Left', *Journal of the Association for Contemporary Iberian Studies*, vol. 5, no. 2 (London, Autumn 1992), pp. 40–51. Challenges the generally accepted view that the Left lost the 1933 elections primarily as a result of disunion. See also [25].

[16] A. Durgan, *B.O.C., El Bloque Obrero y Campesino, 1930–1936* (Barcelona, 1996). Places the history of the dissident communist BOC within the context of the Catalan workers' movement. See also [17].

[17] A. Durgan, 'The Search for Unity: Marxists and the Trade-Union Movement in Barcelona, 1931–6', in Smith, *Red Barcelona: Social Protest*, cited in [6]. On Barcelona's little-studied non-anarchist labour movement. See also [19].

[18] C. Ealham, 'From the Summit to the Abyss: the Contradictions of Individualism and Collectivism in Spanish Anarchism', in P. Preston and A. L. Mackenzie (eds), *The Republic Besieged: Civil War in Spain, 1936–1939* (Edinburgh, 1996). Discusses the weaknesses and contradictions in pre-war anarchist ideology, in particular the 'culture of indiscipline' and its consequences in the Civil War. See also [143].

[19] C. Ealham, 'The Crisis of Organised Labour: the Battle for Hegemony in the Barcelona Workers' Movement, 1930–6', in Smith, *Red Barcelona: Social Protest*, cited in [6]. On the divisions inside the pre-war Barcelona labour movement, see also [17].

[20] C. Ealham, *Class, Conflict and Culture in Barcelona, 1898–1937* (London, 2004). Highly original account of the social and cultural basis of anarchism and popular resistance in pre-war Barcelona. Indispensable. Contrast with [143] and [168].

[21] J. P. Fusi, 'Centre and Periphery, 1900–1936: National Integration and Regional Nationalisms Reconsidered', in Lannon and Preston, *Elites and Power*, cited in [4]. Useful analysis of the national question in early twentieth-century Spain. See also [13] and [44].

[22] P. C. González Cuevas, *Acción Española. Teología política y nacionalismo autoritario en España (1913–1937)* (Madrid, 1998). The theoretical basis and origins of National Catholicism. See also [35].

Bibliography

[23] P. Heywood, *Marxism and the Failure of Organised Socialism in Spain, 1879–1936* (Cambridge, 1990). Fundamental analysis of the PSOE's Marxism and political practice during the Second Republic.

[24] S. Holguín, *Creating Spaniards. Culture and National Identity in Republican Spain* (Madison, Wis., 2002). One of the few studies that deals with the politics of culture in 1930s Spain and attempts to forge a national identity. See also [11] and [69].

[25] W. J. Irwin, *The 1933 Cortes Elections: Origin of the Bienio Negro* (New York, 1991). The only detailed study of these crucial elections. See also [15].

[26] S. Juliá, 'Economic Crisis, Social Conflict and the Popular Front: Madrid, 1931–6', in P. Preston (ed.), *Revolution and War in Spain, 1931–1939* (London, 2001). Resume of important work on the socio-political history of Madrid and origins of the Popular Front. See also [46].

[27] S. Juliá, 'The Origins and Nature of the Spanish Popular Front', in Alexander and Graham, *The French and Spanish Popular Fronts*, cited in [1]. Adds to [26].

[28] G. Kelsley, *Anarchosyndicalism, Libertarian Communism and the State: The CNT in Zaragosa and Aragon, 1930–1938* (Amsterdam, 1991). Detailed study of Aragonese anarcho-syndicalism and background to the revolution.

[29] F. Lannon, *Privilege, Persecution and Prophecy: The Catholic Church in Spain, 1875–1975* (Oxford, 1987). Classic study, combining social and political history of the Church. See also [7] and [187].

[30] E. Malefakis, *Agrarian Reform and Peasant Revolution in Spain* (London, 1970). Major study of the agrarian problem and attempted reform during the Republic. See also [42].

[31] T. Mitchell, *Betrayal of the Innocents: Desire, Power and the Catholic Church in Spain* (Philadelphia, 1998). From the standpoint of psychoanalysis and social psychology, seeks to demonstrate that male sexuality is the key to understanding the behaviour of the clergy and its enemies.

[32] S. Payne, *Spain's First Democracy* (Madison, 1993). Blames leftist contempt for legality, for the collapse of democracy and the advent of war. Contrast with [36].

[33] S. Payne, *The Collapse of the Spanish Republic, 1933–1936: Origins of the Civil War* (New Haven, CT, 2006). Follows most of the recent revisionist histories. See also [32] and [67].

[34] M. Perez Ledesma, 'Studies on Anticlericalism in Contemporary Spain', *International Review of Social History*, 46 (Amsterdam, 2001) pp. 227–55. Very useful overview and discussion of the origins of anticlericalism. See also [14] and [171].

[35] P. Preston, *The Politics of Revenge: Fascism and the Military in 20th-Century Spain* (London, 1990). Essays on the Right and the military.

[36] P. Preston, *The Coming of the Spanish Civil War: Reform, Reaction and Revolution in the Second Republic* (London, 1994). Seminal political history of the Republic; centres on its two main parties, the PSOE and CEDA, demonstrating the latter's responsibility for the Republic's collapse; contrast with [32] and [33].

135

[37] P. Preston, 'The Agrarian War in the South', in Preston, *Revolution and War in Spain*, cited in [26]. Shows the centrality of the agrarian problem to the war's origins. See also [12] and [30].

[38] P. Preston, *Comrades* (London, 1999). Collection of biographies of nine leading figures of the period. With a final chapter on the 'third' Spain.

[39] P. Preston, *Doves of War* (London, 2002). Biographies of four women protagonists.

[40] P. B. Radcliff, *From Mobilisation to Civil War: The Politics of Polarisation in the Spanish City of Gijon, 1900–1937* (Cambridge, 1996). Innovative case study of one northern industrial city showing the inter-relationship between class, culture, ideology and social polarisation leading towards war.

[41] T. Rees, 'Women on the Land: Household and Work in the Southern Countryside, 1875–1939', in V. L. Enders and P. B. Radcliff (eds), *Construction of Spanish Womanhood: Female Identity in Modern Spain* (New York, 1999). Looks at neglected area of the overlap between women's domestic and non-domestic labour and how this shaped both the rural economy and gender roles.

[42] J. Rodríguez Labandeira, *El trabajo rural en España (1876–1936)* (Barcelona, 1991). Very thorough and well-documented account of rural work and labour relations. See also [30].

[43] A. Shubert, *The Road to Revolution in Spain: The Coal Miners of Asturias, 1860–1934* (Chicago, 1987). Impressive study that shows the socio-economic roots of the radicalisation of Asturian miners.

[44] A. Smith and C. Mar-Molinero, 'The Myths and Realities of Nation-Building in the Iberian Peninsula', in C. Mar-Molinero and A. Smith (eds), *Nationalism and the Nation in the Iberian Peninsula* (Oxford, 1996). Clear and contextualised analysis of the rise of peripheral nationalisms. See also [13] and [21].

[45] A. Soto Carmona, *El trabajo industrial en la España contemporánea (1874–1936)* (Barcelona, 1989). Exhaustive study of working conditions and labour relations in pre-war industry. Complement to [42] and [48].

[46] S. Souto Kustrín, *"Y ¡Madrid? ¿Qué hace Madrid?" Movimiento revolucionario y acción colectiva (1933–1936)* (Madrid, 2004). Only study of the background and consequences of October 1934 in Madrid. See also [26].

[47] S. Souto Kustrín, 'Taking the Street: Workers' Youth Organizations and Political Conflict in the Spanish Second Republic', *European History Quarterly*, 34 (London, April 2004), pp. 131–56. Much-needed contribution on the role of youth organisation in the process of radicalisation.

[48] G. Tortella, *The Development of Modern Spain: An Economic History of the Nineteenth and Twentieth Centuries* (Cambridge, Mass., 2000). Classic economic history. See also [42] and [45].

[49] N. Townson, *The Crisis of Democracy in Spain: Centrist Politics under the Second Republic, 1931–1936* (Brighton, 2000). The only documented

history of the Radical Party and the failure to establish a viable political centre.

[50] M. Vincent, *Catholicism in the Second Spanish Republic: Religion and Politics in Salamanca, 1930–1936* (Oxford, 1996). Notable case-study that illustrates the relationship between the Church and the Right during the Republic.

General and Military Histories of the Civil War

[51] M. Alpert, 'La historia militar', in S. Payne and J. Tusell, *La guerra civil: Una nueva visión del conflicto que dividio España* (Madrid, 1996). Excellent summary of the military history of the war. See also [52], [54], [57] and [72].

[52] M. Alpert, 'The Clash of Spanish Armies: Contrasting Ways of War in Spain, 1936–1939', *War in History*, nol. 6, no. 3 (Oxford, 1999), pp. 331–51. Outstanding comparative discussion of the different military strategies and composition of the competing armies.

[53] J. Aróstegui and F. Godicheau (eds), *Guerra Civil. Mito y Memoria* (Madrid, 2006). Interesting collection of essays on memory and historiography. See also [73].

[54] A. Beevor, *Battle for Spain: The Spanish Civil War, 1936–1939* (London, 2006). Updated general history, particularly strong on the military side.

[55] W. L. Bernecker, *Guerra en España, 1936–1939* (Madrid, 1996). Very useful overview of historiographical debates.

[56] P. Broué and E. Témime, *The Revolution and Civil War in Spain* (London, 1972). Classic Marxist account.

[57] G. Cardona, *Historia militar de una guerra civil* (Barcelona, 2006). Concise military history. See also [51] and [72].

[58] R. Carr, *The Spanish Tragedy: Civil War in Perspective* (London, 2002). Notable interpretive account.

[59] J. Casanova, 'Civil Wars, Revolutions and Counterrevolutions in Finland, Spain and Greece (1918–1949): a Comparative Analysis', *International Journal of Politics, Culture and Society*, vol. 13, no. 3 (March, 2000), pp. 515–37. Interesting comparison of the Franco dictatorship with other authoritarian regimes that emerged from civil wars.

[60] C. Ealham and M. Richards (eds), *The Splintering of Spain, 1936–1945: Cultural History and the Spanish Civil War* (Cambridge, 2005). Innovative essays on different aspects of the cultural history of the war with a very useful introductory chapter on recent historiography.

[61] G. Esenwein, *The Spanish Civil War: Spain's Experience of Domestic Conflict and Revolution in the 20th Century* (London, 2005). Collection of extracts from primary sources with instructive historiographical introduction.

[62] R. Fraser, *Blood of Spain: An Oral History of the Spanish Civil War* (London, 1994). Unsurpassed oral history of the war.

Bibliography

[63] H. Graham, *The Spanish Civil War: A Very Short Introduction* (Oxford, 2005). Excellent thought-provoking short introduction.

[64] S. Juliá (et al.), *Víctimas de la Guerra Civil* (Madrid, 1999). Essays on repression based on local studies. See also [175], [180] and [188].

[65] A. Kenwood (ed.), *The Spanish Civil War: A Cultural and Historical Reader* (Oxford, 1993). Representative selection of essays and extracts from different sources. See also [109].

[66] E. Malefakis, 'Balance final', in E. Malefakis (ed.), *La guerra de España 1936–1939* (Madrid, 2006). Interesting reflection on the causes and course of the war.

[67] P. Moa, *Los mitos de la Guerra Civil* (Madrid, 2004). Top-selling revisionist account. Contrast with [68].

[68] E. Moradiellos, *1936: Los mitos de la Guerra Civil* (Barcelona, 2004). Eloquent riposte to revisionists.

[69] X. Núñez Seixas, 'Nations in Arms against the Invader: on Nationalist Discourses during the Spanish Civil War', in Ealham and Richards, see [60]. Compares Nationalist discourse of both sides. See also [24].

[70] S. de Pablo, 'La guerra civil en el País Vasco: ¿un conflicto diferente?' in E. Moradiellos (ed.), *La Guerra Civil. Ayer*, no. 50 (Madrid, 2003), pp. 115–42. Good summary of war in the Basque Country.

[71] P. Preston, *The Spanish Civil War: Reaction, Revolution and Revenge* (London, 2006). Updated, re-written and extended version of the author's excellent earlier work on the war.

[72] R. L. Proctor, 'A Military History of the Spanish Civil War: 1936–1939', in J. W. Cortada (ed.), *Historical Dictionary of the Spanish Civil War, 1936–39* (London, 1982). Summary of military operations; sympathetic to the Nationalists. Compare with [51] and [57].

[73] R. Rein (ed.), *Spanish Memories: Images of a Contested Past; History and Memory*, vol. 14 (Bloomington, Ind., Fall 2002). Recent work on memory. See also [53].

[74] F. Ribeiro de Meneses, *Franco and the Spanish Civil War* (London, 2001). Introductory history with a useful final chapter on the contenders' different visions of Spain.

[75] F. J. Romero Salvado, *The Spanish Civil War: Origins, Course and Outcomes* (Basingstoke, 2005). Lucid and updated introductory history.

[76] J. Ruiz Portella (ed.), *La Guerra Civil: ¿dos o tres Españas?* (Barcelona, 1999). Essays on the 'third Spain'. See also [38].

[77] H. Thomas, *The Spanish Civil War* (Harmondsworth, 2001). Classic general history, first published in 1961 and subsequently revised and extended.

The International Dimension

[78] M. Alpert, *A New International History of the Spanish Civil War* (London, 2004). Excellent general account of the international dimension.

Bibliography

[79] M. Alpert, 'The Spanish Civil War and the Mediterranean', *Mediterranean Historical Review*, 13, 1–2 (Tel Aviv, 1998), pp. 150–67. Key essay on Mussolini's ambitions in the western Mediterranean, Britain's response and the consequences for the Republic. See also [94].

[80] S. Balfour, *Deadly Embrace: Morocco and the Road to the Spanish Civil War* (Oxford, 2002). Excellent account of Spain's colonial presence in Morocco and the making of the Army of Africa. See also [92] and [107].

[81] R. Baxell, *British Volunteers in the Spanish Civil War* (London, 2004). Definitive history of the British Battalion which points to the Popular Frontist character of the International Brigades. See also [96].

[82] W. H. Bowen, *Spaniards and Nazi Germany: Collaboration in the New Order* (Columbia, Miss., 2000). On the relationship of Spaniards with the Nazi regime.

[83] P. Broué, *Staline et la révolution: le cas espagnol* (Paris, 1993). Stalin as gravedigger of the Spanish revolution. Contrast with [102], [120] and [121].

[84] T. Buchanan, *Britain and the Spanish Civil War* (Cambridge, 1997). British reactions to the war, from foreign policy through to public opinion and solidarity. See also [85] and [111].

[85] T. Buchanan, *The Spanish Civil War and the British Labour Movement* (Cambridge, 1991). Detailed study of the twists and turns of British labour in relation to the Spanish war. See also [96].

[86] P. N. Carroll, *The Odyssey of the Abraham Lincoln Brigade: Americans in the Spanish Civil War* (Stanford, 1994). Excellent history of the American volunteers, their motivations for going, experience of war and subsequent ostracism, and solidarity work.

[87] N. Cerdá, 'The Road to Dunkirk: British Intelligence and the Spanish Civil War', *War in History*, vol. 13, no. 1 (Oxford, January 2006) pp. 42–64. How stereotypes and inter-service struggles prevented the British armed forces from learning from the Civil War.

[88] J. S. Corum, 'The Spanish Civil War: Lessons Learned and Not Learned by the Great Powers', *Journal of Military History*, vol. 62, no. 2 (Lexington, 1998), pp. 313–34. How the major powers analysed the air war in Spain.

[89] A. Elorza and M. Bizcarrondo, *Queridos camaradas. La Internacional Comunista y España, 1919–1939* (Barcelona, 1999). Very critical view of Comintern activity in Spain, based on material from the Moscow archives. See also [114] and [120].

[90] M. Falcoff and F. B. Pike (eds), *Spanish Civil War: American Hemispheric Perspectives* (Lincoln/London, 1982). Essays on the different American responses to the war. See also [113].

[91] W. C. Frank, 'The Spanish Civil War and the Coming of the Second World War', *International History Review*, 9 (Burnaby, DC, 1987), pp. 368–409. Well-researched discussion of great power interventions in Spain and their relation to the coming world war. See also [93].

[92] J. A. González Alcantud (ed.), *Marroquíes en la guerra civil española.*

Campos equívocos (Granada, 2003). Instructive collection of essays on different aspects of Moroccan participation. See also [80] and [107].

[93] M. Habeck, 'The Spanish Civil War and the Origins of the Second World War', in G. Martel (ed.), *The Origins of the Second World War Reconsidered, Second Edition: A. J. P. Taylor and the Historians* (London, 1999). Despite using German and Russian sources, the absence of references to major studies in English and Spanish undermines this potentially interesting essay. See also [91].

[94] M. Heiberg, *Emperadores del mediterráneo. Franco, Mussolini y la guerra civil española* (Barcelona, 2003). Based on previously unused sources, this excellent study argues that Mussolini's policy in Spain was even more ambitious than has previously been thought. See also [117].

[95] M. Heiberg and M. Pelt, *Los negocios de la Guerra: Armas nazis para la Republica española* (Barcelona, 2005). Fascinating account of the sale of Nazi arms to the Republic through Greek intermediaries. See also [97].

[96] J. K. Hopkins, *Into the Heart of the Fire: The British in the Spanish Civil War* (Stanford, 1998). Account of British International Brigade volunteers, strong on context, motives and the role of intellectuals. See also [81].

[97] G. Howson, *Arms for Spain* (London, 1998). Highly original research on how the Republic armed itself; demonstrates how the Soviet government overcharged for the arms by manipulating exchange rates. See also [95]. Contrast with [102].

[98] A. Jackson, *British Women and the Spanish Civil War* (Routledge, 2002). Detailed account of British women with the International Brigades.

[99] P. Jackson, 'French Strategy and the Spanish Civil War', in C. Leitz and D. J. Dunthorn (eds), *Spain in an International Context, 1936–1959* (Oxford, 1999). How the French General Staff opposed intervention in Spain for strategic reasons.

[100] J. Keene, *Fighting for Franco: International Volunteers in Nationalist Spain during the Spanish Civil War* (London, 2003). Unique study of foreign volunteers on the Nationalist side.

[101] C. Kent, 'The Vatican and the Spanish Civil War', *European History Quarterly*, 16, no. 4 (London, 1986), pp. 441–64. Essay on the little-studied question of the Vatican's reaction to the Civil War.

[102] D. Kowalsky, *La Unión Soviética y la Guerra Civil Española* (Barcelona, 2004). Important study based on Soviet archive material; argues that Stalin's intervention in Spain was contradictory and incompetent rather than malevolent. On-line version available in English. Contrast with [89]. See also [118].

[103] C. Leitz, *The Economic Relations between Nazi Germany and Franco's Spain, 1936–45* (Oxford, 1996). Thoroughly researched study; shows how Nazi Germany maximised the economic advantages of its relationship with Nationalist Spain. See also [133].

[104] D. Little, 'Red Scare, 1936: Anti-Bolshevism and the Origins of British Non-Intervention in the Spanish Civil War', *Journal of Contemporary History*, vol. 23 (London, 1988), pp. 291–311. Interesting

Bibliography

essay on the role of anti-Communism behind British Non-Intervention.

[105] D. Little, *Malevolent Neutrality: The United States, Great Britain and the Origins of Non-Intervention* (Ithaca, NY, 1985). How both the British and US governments' hostility to the Republic in the pre-war years led to Non-Intervention. See also [112].

[106] C. C. Locksley, 'Condor over Spain: the Civil War, Combat Experience and the Development of the Luftwaffe Airpower Doctrine', in *Civil Wars*, vol. 2, no. 1 (London, Spring 1999), pp. 69–99. On the importance of the Civil War experience for the Luftwaffe's future strategy. See also [88].

[107] M. R. de Madariaga, 'The Intervention of Moroccan Troops in the Spanish Civil War: a Reconsideration', *European History Quarterly*, 22 (London, 1992), pp. 67–97. Pioneering study on the recruitment and role of Moroccan troops. See also [80] and [92].

[108] R. Miralles, 'The International Policy of the Second Republic during the Spanish Civil War', *Mediterranean Historical Review*, vol. 13, 1/2 (Tel Aviv, June/December 1998), pp. 135–49. Analyses diplomatic moves by the Republic to counter Non-Intervention.

[109] P. Monteath, *Writing the Good Fight: Political Commitment in the International Literature of the Spanish Civil War* (Westport, 1994). A good survey of international literature on the war. See also [65].

[110] E. Moradiellos, 'The Gentle General: the Official British Perception of General Franco during the Spanish Civil War', in Preston and Mackenzie, *The Republic Besieged*, cited in [18]. On how the Foreign Office perceived Franco.

[111] E. Moradiellos, 'The British Government and General Franco during the Spanish Civil War', in Leitz and Dunthorn (eds), *Spain in an International Context*, cited in [99]. Reflects this historian's important work in Spanish. See also [110] and [112].

[112] E. Moradiellos, 'The Allies and the Spanish Civil War', in S. Balfour and P. Preston (eds), *Spain and the Great Powers* (London, 1999). Excellent updated overview. See also [105] and [111].

[113] M. Ojeda Revah, *México y la Guerra Civil Española* (Madrid, 2004). Important new study; challenges existing understanding of Mexico's policy regarding the Spanish war. Contrast with [90].

[114] S. Payne, *The Spanish Civil War, the Soviet Union and Communism* (New Haven, CT, 2004). Argues that Soviet policy in Spain aimed at establishing a Communist regime. Contrast with [102], [120] and [121].

[115] S. Payne, 'Fascist Italy and Spain, 1922–45', *Mediterranean Historical Review*, vol. 13, 1/2 (Tel Aviv, June/December 1998), pp. 99–115. Covers the different phases of fascist Italy's relationship with Spain. Contrast with [117].

[116] P. Preston, 'Mussolini's Spanish Adventure: from Limited Risk to War', in Preston and Mackenzie, *The Republic Besieged*, cited in [18]. Challenges the standard view of how Mussolini was persuaded to intervene.

141

[117] P. Preston, 'Italy and Spain in Civil War and World War 1936–1943', in Balfour and Preston, *Spain and the Great Powers*, cited in [112]. Important contribution to our understanding of Italian motives and policy towards Nationalist Spain. See also [94].

[118] R. Radosh, M. R. Habek and G. Sevostianov (eds), *Spain Betrayed: The Soviet Union in the Spanish Civil War* (London/New Haven, 2001). Collection of previously unedited Soviet documents; despite poor editing, includes some extremely important material. See also [89] and [114].

[119] A. Raya-Rivas, 'An Iberian Alliance: Portuguese Intervention in the Spanish Civil War (1936–1939)', *Portuguese Studies Review*, vol. III, no. 1 (Durham, New Hampshire, Fall–winter 1999–2000), pp. 109–25. One of the few studies in English on the question. See also [78] and [125].

[120] T. Rees, 'The Highpoint of Comintern Influence? The Communist Party and the Civil War in Spain', in T. Rees and A. Thorpe (eds), *International Communism and the Communist International, 1919–1943* (Manchester, 1998). Using Soviet archive material, argues that the Soviet government was incapable of controlling events in Spain even if it had wanted to. Contrast with [89] and [114].

[121] G. Roberts, 'Soviet Foreign Policy and the Spanish Civil War 1936–1939', in Leitz and Dunthorn, *Spain in an International Context*, cited in [99]. On how Soviet policy was inspired by anti-Fascism. Compare with [124].

[122] I. Saz, 'Fascism and Empire: Fascist Italy against the Second Republic', *Mediterranean Historical Review*, vol. 13, 1/2 (Tel Aviv, June/December 1998), pp. 116–33. On the relation between foreign and internal Italian fascist policy aims and intervention in Spain. See also [94], [115] and [117].

[123] R. Skoutelsky, *Novedad en el frente. Las Brigadas Internacionales en la guerra civil* (Madrid, 2006). Best general history of the Brigades yet to be published; thoroughly researched and including newly available archive material.

[124] D. Smyth, 'We are with You: Solidarity and Self-interest in Soviet Policy towards Republican Spain, 1936–1939', in Preston and Mackenzie, *The Republic Besieged*, cited in [18]. On how Stalin's policy in Spain was subordinated to the need to achieve collective security. Contrast with [121].

[125] G. Stone, *Spain, Portugal and the Great Powers, 1931–1941* (Basingstoke, 2005). Useful new overview.

[126] R. Stradling, *The Irish and the Spanish Civil War, 1936–1939* (Manchester, 1999). Good survey of Irish views and involvement on both sides of the war.

[127] R. Stradling, *Wales and the Spanish Civil War: The Dragon's Dearest Cause* (Cardiff, 2004). Interesting study of solidarity with and volunteers for the Republican cause.

[128] R. S. Thornberry, 'Writers Take Sides, Stalinists Take Control: the Second International Congress for the Defence of Culture', *The*

Bibliography

Historian (East Lansing, Mich., Spring 2000), pp. 589–605. On Communist influence among writers internationally.

[129] D. Tierney, 'Franklin D. Roosevelt and Covert Aid to the Loyalists in the Spanish Civil War, 1936–39', *Journal of Contemporary History*, 39 (London, July 2004), pp. 299–313. Essay that examines the possibility that Roosevelt was considering sending aid to the Republic in the later stages of the war.

[130] R. Veatch, 'The League of Nations and the Spanish Civil War 1936–9', *European History Quarterly*, 20, 2 (London, 1990), pp. 181–207. One of the few studies on the abandonment of the Republic by the League of Nations.

[131] A. Viñas, *Franco, Hitler y el estallido de la Guerra Civil* (Madrid, 2001). Authoritative study of Hitler's motives for intervening in Spain. See also [103] and [133].

[132] A. Viñas and C. Collado Seidel, 'Franco's Request to the Third Reich for Military Assistance', *Contemporary European History*, vol. 11, 2 (Cambridge, 2002) pp. 191–210. New revelations on the process that led Hitler to intervene.

[133] R. H. Whealy, *Hitler and Spain* (Lexington, Ken., 1989). Fundamental study on Nazi policy in the Civil War. See also [103] and [131].

[134] S. J. Zaloga, 'Soviet Tank Operations in the Spanish Civil War', *Journal of Slavic Military Studies*, vol. 12, no. 3 (London, September 1999), pp. 134–62. Detailed essay on Soviet tank operations and strategy.

The Republican Zone

[135] M. A. Ackelsberg, *Free Women of Spain: Anarchism and the Struggle for the Emancipation of Women* (Bloomington, Ind., 1991). Written from a feminist perspective, the only substantial study of *Mujeres Libres*. See also [150] and [162].

[136] A. Alted, 'The Republican and Nationalist Wartime Cultural Apparatus', in H. Graham and J. Labanyi, *Spanish Cultural Studies: An Introduction* (Oxford, 1995). Interesting short essay on this little-studied area. See also [24].

[137] J. Arostegui, 'Guerra poder y revolución. La República española y el impacto de la sublevación', in Moradiellos, *La Guerra Civil*, cited in [70], pp. 85–114. Useful updated overview of the war in the Republican zone.

[138] W. L. Bernecker, 'La revolución social', in Payne and Tusell, *La guerra civil*, cited in [51]. Excellent essay by one of the foremost specialists on the social revolution.

[139] B. Bolloten and G. Esenwein, 'Anarchists in Government: a Paradox of the Spanish Civil War, 1936–1939', in Lannon and Preston, *Elites and Power*, cited in [4]. Reasons behind and consequences of anarchist participation in government.

[140] B. Bolloten, *The Spanish Civil War: Revolution and Counterrevolution*

143

(Hemel Hempstead, 1991). Controversial and monumental study of the Communist role in the war, extensively revised by its author over the years; argues strongly that Stalinist policy was responsible for the Republic's defeat. Contrast with [153].

[141]   A. Bosch, 'Collectivisations: the Spanish Revolution Revisited, 1936–1939', *International Journal of Iberian Studies*, vol. 14, 1 (London, 2001). Covers the unique collectivist experience in the Valencia region. See also [142].

[142]   J. Casanova (ed.), *El sueño igualitario* (Zaragoza, 1988). Useful collection of essays on collectivisation.

[143]   J. Casanova, *Anarchists and the Spanish Civil War* (London, 2004). Critical account, based on a broad range of recent studies and research, of the contradictory role of the anarchists, written from a markedly Popular Front perspective. Contrast with [164].

[144]   A. Castells, 'Revolution and collectivisation in Civil War Barcelona, 1936–9', in Smith, *Red Barcelona. Social Protest*, cited in [6]. Discusses the nature of the collectivisation process in Barcelona and its eventual bringing under state control.

[145]   J. Corbin, 'Truth and Myth in History: an Example from the Spanish Civil War', *Journal of Interdisciplinary History*, XXV, 4 (Cambridge, Mass., Spring 1995), pp. 609–25. Fascinating deconstruction of supposed rearguard atrocity cited in many standard works.

[146]   J. de la Cueva, 'Religious Persecution, Anticlerical Tradition and Revolution: on Atrocities against the Clergy during the Spanish Civil War', *Journal of Contemporary History*, vol. 33, no. 3 (London, 1998), pp. 355–69. Essay on anti-clerical repression based, in part, on Francoist sources. See also [34] and [171]. Contrast with [148] and [174].

[147]   A. Durgan, 'Marxism, War and Revolution: Trotsky and the POUM', *Stalinism, Revolution and Counter-Revolution: Revolutionary History* vol. 9, no. 2 (London, 2006) pp. 27–65. Nuanced and contextualised account of Trotsky's critique of the POUM.

[148]   C. Ealham, 'The Myth of the Maddened Crowd: Class, Culture and Space in the Revolutionary Urbanist Project in Barcelona, 1936–1937', in Ealham and Richards, *The Splintering of Spain*, see [60]. Superb essay on the battle for and transformation of urban space in revolutionary Barcelona. See also [20].

[149]   F. Godicheau, *La Guerre d'Espagne. République et Révolution en Catalogne (1936–1939)* (Paris, 2004). Includes important new work on the much-neglected question of repression in Republican Catalonia after May 1937.

[150]   M. A. Gómez, 'Feminism and Anarchism: Remembering the Role of Mujeres Libres in the Spanish Civil War', in L. Vollendorf, *Recovering Spain's Feminist Tradition* (New York, 2001). Includes sections on the film *Libertarias* and the memoirs of activist Sara Berenguer. See also [135] and [162].

[151]   H. Graham, *Socialism and War: The Spanish Socialist Party in Power and Crisis, 1936–1939* (Cambridge, 1991). The only study of the Socialist movement during the war.

Bibliography

[152] H. Graham, 'Women and Social Change', in Graham and Labanyi, *Spanish Cultural Studies*, cited in [136]. Good summary of the situation facing women during the Republic and war. See also [162].

[153] H. Graham, *The Spanish Republic at War, 1936–1939* (Cambridge, 2002). One of the most important contributions to recent historiography; extremely well-documented study locates the development of Republican politics in the context of the war and long-standing socio-political divisions; provides a sophisticated defence of the Popular Front and a re-evaluation of the role of the Communist Party. Contrast with [140].

[154] A. Guillamon, *The Friends of Durruti Group, 1937–1939* (Edinburgh/San Francisco, 1996). One of the few serious studies of this little-understood anarchist group.

[155] M. Hughes and E. Garrido, 'Planning and Command: the Spanish Republican Army and the Battle of the Ebro, 1938', *International Journal of Iberian Studies*, vol. 12, no. 2 (London, 1999), pp. 125–43. With the Ebro as a case study, emphasises the difficulties that the Republic had in creating a modern army capable of winning the war. See also [52].

[156] J. Keene, 'No More than Brothers and Sisters: Women in Front Line Combat in the Spanish Civil War', in P. Monteath and F. S. Zuckerman (eds), *Modern Europe: Histories and Identities* (Adelaide, 1998). See also [162].

[157] J. Labanyi, 'Propaganda Art: Culture By the People or For the People?' in Graham an Labanyi, *Spanish Cultural Studies*, cited in [136]. Interesting short study on the relation between art and propaganda.

[158] J. McCarthy, *Political Theatre during the Spanish Civil War* (Cardiff, 1999). One of the few studies of the role of political theatre in the war.

[159] R. Maddox, 'Revolutionary Anticlericalism and Hegemonic Processes in an Andalusian Town, August 1936', *American Ethnologist*, 22 (Berkeley, Cal., 1995), pp. 125–43. Case study of one town that shows there was not just one cause of anti-clerical violence. See also [34]. Contrast with [146].

[160] S. Mangini, *Memories of Resistance: Women's Voices from the Spanish Civil War* (New Haven/London, 1995). Study of women's experience of social change, war and repression based on memory-texts.

[161] J. Martínez-Gutiérrez, 'Margarita Nelken: Feminist and Political Praxis during the Spanish Civil War', in Vollendorf, *Recovering Spain's Feminist Tradition*, cited in [150]. Short essay on the most interesting female left-wing leader of the time. See also [38].

[162] M. Nash, *Defying Male Civilisation: Women in the Spanish Civil War* (Denver, 1995). Only overall study of women in the Republican zone, which both questions established myths and contextualises the changes in many women's lives.

[163] A. Paz, *The Iron Column: Militant Anarchism in the Spanish Civil War* (London, 2006). Sympathetic study of the most radical of anarchist militia columns.

[164]   J. Peirats, *The CNT in the Spanish Revolution*, 3 vols (Hastings, 2001/2006). Classic anarchist version of events, in English for the first time, with excellent explanatory footnotes and introduction by C. Ealham. Contrast with [143].

[165]   G. Orwell, *Orwell in Spain* (London, 2001). Complete collection of Orwell's writings on Spain, including *Homage to Catalonia*, one of the most influential books published in English on the war.

[166]   P. Radcliff, 'The Culture of Empowerment in Gijón, 1936–1937', in Ealham and Richards, *The Splintering of Spain*, see [60]. Examines the overlapping political and social identities of the Republic's urban base. See also [40].

[167]   R. Salas Larrazábal, 'The Growth and Role of the Republican Popular Army', in R. Carr (ed.), *The Republic and the Civil War* (London, 1971). Summary of the major study of the Republican Army by one of the more competent regime historians. Contrast with [52].

[168]   M. Seidman, *Workers Against Work: Labor in Paris and Barcelona during the Popular Fronts* (Berkeley/Oxford, 1991). Argues that as workers continued to reject work under the Popular Front they had to be coerced to support the war effort.

[169]   M. Seidman, *Republic of Egos: A Social History of the Spanish Civil War* (Madison, Wis., 2002). Based on rarely used military archive material, this controversial study attempts of show the dominance of individualist and consumerist rather than collective values in the Republican rearguard.

[170]   E. Ucelay-Da-Cal, 'Catalan Populism in the Spanish Civil War', in Ealham and Richards, *The Splintering of Spain*, see [60]. On the Catalan Left and inter-class populism during the war.

[171]   M. Vincent, '"The keys to the kingdom": Religious Violence in the Spanish Civil War, July–August 1936', in Ealham and Richards, *The Splintering of Spain*, see [60]. Interesting reflections on the nature of anti-clerical violence. See also [146]. Contrast with [148] and [174].

The Nationalist Zone

[172]   G. Ashford Hodges, *Franco: A Concise Biography* (New York, 2002). Fascinating psychological portrait of the dictator. See also [185].

[173]   C. Blanco Escola, *La incompetencia militar de Franco* (Madrid, 2000). Demolition of the military myth of Franco by a former army officer. See also [186].

[174]   J. Casanova, *La iglesia de Franco* (Madrid, 2001). Vibrant exposé of the Church as the active promoter and defender of Franco's dictatorship rather than a passive victim of anti-clerical outrage. Contrast, in part, with [7] and [187].

[175]   J. Casanova, 'Una dictadura de cuarenta años', in J. Casanova (ed.), *Morir, matar, sobrevivir. La violencia en la dictadura de Franco* (Barcelona, 2002). Excellent and informed essay on the politics and practice of repression in the Nationalist rearguard. See also [64] and [180].

[176]   Á. Cenarro, 'Instituciones y poder local en el "Nuevo Estado"', in S. Juliá (ed.), *República y Guerra en España (1931–1939)* (Madrid, 2006). Interesting new study on the construction of the new state at a local level.

[177]   R. Cruz, 'Old Symbols, New Meanings: Mobilising the Rebellion in the Summer of 1936', in Ealham and Richards, *The Splintering of Spain*, see [60]. On how the Monarchist flag and the concept of the religious crusade were used to sustain Nationalist mobilisation.

[178]   S. Ellwood, *Spanish Fascism in the Franco Era: Falange Española de las JONs* (London, 1988). Pioneering and thoroughly researched history of the Falange. See also [197].

[179]   V. L. Enders, 'Problematic Portraits: the Ambiguous Historical Role of the *Sección Feminina* of the Falange', in Enders and Radcliff, *Construction of Spanish Womanhood*, cited in [41]. Discusses the contradictions between the SF's defence of traditional subordinate feminine role models and its cadres' projection as public figures. See also [183] and [191].

[180]   F. Espinosa, 'Golpe miltitar y plan de exterminio', in Casanova, *Morir, matar, sobrevivir*, cited in [175]. The role and nature of Nationalist repression as part of a larger extermination policy. Fundamental. See also [64].

[181]   M. Heiberg and M. Ros Aguado, *La trama oculta de la Guerra Civil. Los servicios secretos de Franco, 1936–1945* (Barcelona, 2006). Impressive new work on the rarely studied Nationalist secret services.

[182]   F. Lannon, 'Women and Images of Women in the Spanish Civil War', *Transactions of the Royal Historical Society*, 6th series, 1 (London, 1991) pp. 213–28. Comparative analysis of the different images of women in both zones.

[183]   I. Ofer, 'The Sección Femenina of the Spanish Falange and its Redefinition of the Term "Femininity"', *Journal of Contemporary History*, vol. 40, no. 4 (London, October 2005), pp. 663–74. On how the SF constructed a new discourse on femininity. See also [179] and [191].

[184]   S. Payne, *Fascism in Spain 1923–1977* (Madison, 1999). Much revised standard history of Spanish fascism. Contrast with [35].

[185]   P. Preston, *Franco* (London, 1993). Definitive and superbly written biography which also provides an incisive history of the regime and its origins.

[186]   P. Preston, 'General Franco as Military Leader', *Transactions of the Royal Historical Society*, 6th series, IV (London, 1994), pp. 21–41. See also [173]. Shows that Franco's military strategy was not just conservative but had a clear aim: the annihilation of the Republic's social base.

[187]   H. Raguer, *The Catholic Church and the Spanish Civil War* (London, 2006). Important critical study of the Church's role in the war by a Catholic historian; available in English for the first time. See also [7] and [29].

[188]   M. Richards, *A Time of Silence: Civil War and the Culture of Repression in*

Franco's Spain, 1936–1945 (Cambridge, 1998). Excellent and thoroughly researched account which places the economics of autarky within the context of widespread repression and the regeneration of Spain. See also [175] and [192]. Contrast with [193].

[189]   M. Richards 'Morality and Biology in the Spanish Civil War: Psychiatrists, Revolution and Women's Prisons in Malaga', *Contemporary European History*, vol. 10, 3 (Cambridge, 2002), pp. 395–421. Fascinating essay on the role of pseudo-scientific experiments on the 'genetic roots of Marxism'.

[190]   M. Richards, ' "Presenting arms to the Blessed Sacrament': Civil War and Semana Santa in the city of Málaga, 1936–1939', in Ealham and Richards, *The Splintering of Spain*, see [60]. Case study which illustrates the role and significance of liturgical ceremonies in building Nationalist identity and underscoring moral regeneration.

[191]   K. Richmond, *Women and Spanish Fascism: The Women's Section of the Falange, 1934–1959* (London, 2003). Serious and well documented history of this important mass organisation. See also [179] and [183].

[192]   J. Rodrigo, *Cautivos. Campos de concentración en la España franquista, 1936–1947* (Barcelona, 2005). Important new study of the Nationalist concentration camp system. See also [175], [188] and [193].

[193]   J. Ruiz, *Franco's Justice: Repression in Madrid after the Spanish Civil War* (Oxford, 2005). Argues that, although harsh, Nationalist repression was not part of a plan to exterminate the Left. Contrast with [180] and [188].

[194]   I. Saz, 'Política en zona nacionalista: la configuración de un régimen', in Moradiellos, *La Guerra Civil*, cited in [70], pp. 55–84. Valuable and updated overview of developments in the Nationalist zone.

[195]   E. Silva, *Las fosas de Franco* (Madrid, 2005). A good example of new studies in the recuperation of historical memory in relation to repression. See also [175].

[196]   H. Southworth, *Conspiracy and the Spanish Civil War. The Brainwashing of Francisco Franco* (London, 2001). A brilliant deconstruction of one of the central justificatory myths of Francoism: the existence of a pre-war Communist plot to launch a revolution.

[197]   J. M. Thomas, *La falange de Franco. El proyecto fascista del régimen* (Barcelona, 2001). New and interesting contribution to the history of the Falange. See also [178].

[198]   J. Tusell, *Franco en la guerra civil. Una biografía política* (Madrid, 2006). Important biography which places Franco in the context of the war. See also [185].

[199]   M. Vincent, 'The Martyrs and the Saints: Masculinity and the Construction of the Francoist Crusade', *History Workshop Journal*, 47 (Cambridge, 1999) pp. 68–98. Looks at the origins of the symbolic images of the crusader and, especially the martyr.

[200]   R. Vinyes (et al.), *Los niños perdidos del franquismo* (Barcelona, 2003). Harrowing account of the forced adoption of the children of Republican prisoners. See also [188].

Index

Index